UNEQUAL JUSTICE

UNEQUAL JUSTICE

Wayne Dumond, Bill Clinton,
and the Politics of Rape in Arkansas

GUY REEL

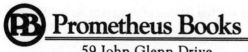

Prometheus Books

59 John Glenn Drive
Buffalo, NewYork 14228-2197

Published 1993 by Prometheus Books

97 96 95 94 93   5 4 3 2 1

Library of Congress Cataloging-in-Publication Data

Reel, Guy.
    Unequal justice : Wayne Dumond, Bill Clinton, and the politics of rape in Arkansas / Guy Reel.
        p.   cm.
    Includes bibliographical references.
    ISBN 0-87975-841-4 (cloth : acid-free paper)
    1. Rape—Arkansas—Forrest City—Case studies.
2. Castration—Case studies. 3. Dumond, Wayne. 4. Police corruption—Arkansas—Forrest City—Case studies. I. Title.
HV6568.F67R44   1993
364.1′32′0976791—dc20   93-28576
                                                            CIP

Printed in the United States of America on acid-free paper.

Prologue

Big city lifestyle is right next door
Our neighbor Memphis has shows galore
Forrest City is what they say
A big little city in the U.S.A.

—A promotional song for Forrest City commissioned
by the Chamber of Commerce at a cost of $48,000

Small-town Arkansas really is bigger than it seems. It's a place of two worlds, one of country club rich, of proper ladies and leisurely golf, of old white men replaying games of checkers at the courthouse square, of boyhood homes of a future president, of manicured lawns and sunset symphonies with champagne fountains. The second world is one of black nightclubs and grinding poverty, teenage pregnancies, and pool-hall killings over welfare checks.

In the middle of the greed-stricken 1980s, when the rich were scrambling to stay ahead of the poor, when the power brokers were deciding who was in charge, there was a strange collision between these two worlds, a collision that would change Arkansas. It was made possible by the intervention of an even stranger hero—a stiff, graying, meticulous newsman who would turn these worlds upside down.

Of course, it must be remembered first that the worlds were not always what they seemed. The "good" white people of the Arkansas South sneaked a few sips of whiskey and downed a few caplets of Valium and crystal meth; the Rotary Club men cheated on their wives; their debutante daughters did it with their boyfriends in the family broughams; and rough-and-tumble allies of the rich and powerful parents committed arson, torture, and murder. The blacks went to church, tilled the fields, and pumped the gas. The good weren't always good, and the bad weren't always bad.

Sound like *Peyton Place* on the farm? Maybe it was— except every word you are about to read is true.

Shall we take a tour of Forrest City, Arkansas, that dusty, grimy, star-crossed Mississippi River Delta town named for a Confederate general and the founder of the Ku Klux Klan? Forrest City was what the Chamber of Commerce claimed was a "big little city in the U.S.A.," as business leaders desperately tried to counteract the horrifying publicity generated by the events recounted in these pages and recruit Japanese industries to replace the dying farm dealers. This East Arkansas town is forty-five miles west of Memphis and the great Mississippi River; it's about one hundred miles east of Little Rock. It may not quite be in the middle of nowhere, but before Bill Clinton parlayed his strength in the Delta into a run for the presidency, the biggest national news for Forrest City came from its election of a gambler sheriff.

Interstate 40 is a black ribbon across the Mississippi River Delta in east Arkansas, cutting across the flat land like a plow row. The Delta is cousin to the Grand Prairie, the great expanse of farmland that stretches across the belly of the state, making it one of the richest agricultural regions in the world. In geologic terms this delta is known as the Mississippi Embayment. By car, cutting through its heart, it amounts to ninety minutes of flat ground. Its counties are uniformly hot in the summer, sitting as it does on the farmland that reflects the sun's heat back up to the sky, rippling the afternoon days away into the humid nights. On clear winter nights in this nowhere, the stars are so bright they can hurt your eyes.

Get off the I-40 exit that takes you into Forrest City and you might notice the Planter's Bank, the bank that lent the sheriff more than half a million dollars. Near the dirty downtown and the Wal-Mart parking lot filled with pickups is a stodgy funeral home with a neat lawn. That was where men looked at another man's cut-out body parts.

Down the street is the courthouse, where the sheriff and his deputies shot high-stakes craps. Out on the highway was a crop-dusting business, owned by the sheriff, which burned down mysteriously in the middle of the night.

Here is the Hungry Rustler, the Holiday Inn; there is a used-car lot that would hire the sheriff; here is the Diamond Burger, with burgers and Cokes to go; there is a lane with fashionable homes and well-trimmed lawns. It was there that a local girl said she was kidnapped by a man and taken out to the woods, where he forced her to perform oral sex until he ejaculated in her mouth. Back down off the highway, there was a funeral home frequented by the blacks of the city, where the politicians came and "gave tithes," and out at the county line, a black nightclub sat, waiting for the nights.

Had a traveler peeked into one of several houses in Forrest City in early 1985, he might have seen a civil rights leader's namesake plotting to burn his own house down, a policeman selling dope, or—on Barrow Hill Road along Crowley's Ridge—men tying up another man and mutilating him into unconsciousness.

Welcome to Forrest City, the seat of St. Francis County. Forrest City, named for the Confederate hero and Ku Klux Klan founder Nathan Bedford Forrest, who established the encampment that became the city. Only the most observant of Forrest City residents would note the irony of Forrest's name occupying such a prominent place in a county named for a saint.

St. Francis of Assisi said, "It behooves us to follow the example of the humility and the poverty of Christ because this is our vocation. And even our tables should be such that if a poor man were invited by the friars, he should sit as their equal and near them, not the poor on the floor and the friars on high."

Well, St. Francis of Assisi never lived in St. Francis County. It was where the poor sat on the dirt like dogs, where the rich ruled over them with iron fists, never expecting scrutiny and never considering the virtues of piety. Yet it was kind of strange: even the wealthy were slaves, in their own way, to power and human means.

This story began, appropriately enough, on an Arkansas backroad stinking of manure. That road twists through the woods of Crowley's Ridge, the low line of hillsides that is the only elevation in the Delta worth talking about. The old station wagon, with a blue Channel 8 TV News logo painted on its side, bounced hard in the deep potholes. Not too far from here were vast soybean and rice fields, the legal cash crops of East Arkansas.

The news car carried TV anchorman Jack Hill and a young black farmer. Hill was there to talk about a story he was working on—the decline of minority farmers, who were being strangled by debt, discrimination, and drought in the hard-luck 1980s. But the young man began to talk about something else: all the gambling and bootlegging in the county and the drug-running in the corrupt city, all under the watchful eye of the high sheriff of St. Francis County, Coolidge Conlee.

"The sheriff knows there's bootlegging?" Hill asked.

The man laughed at him, "Knows? Man, he's the bootlegger!"

Jack Hill had become comfortable at Channel 8, which was based in Jonesboro, about sixty miles northeast of Forrest City. Jonesboro was a progressive, industrial, college town, far more liberal than the backward backwoods of St. Francis County. Here, Hill was the top anchorman on the highest-rated news program in the country. Actually, it was the highest-rated regular program of *any kind* in the nation. Because it had no competition, Channel 8 blanketed the Delta and dominated its market like no other. The viewers of East Arkansas trusted the graying, fatherly, experienced Jack Hill. Everywhere he went he was recognized. People stopped to say hello to him. They waved at him in the grocery store. Strangers wanted to shake his hand.

It seems almost funny, in retrospect, that not too much

later they would laugh in scorn when they heard the name of Jack Hill.

Because it was a small station, Hill had time to pursue reporting, a part of the job he enjoyed. Like all reporters, he settled into a routine. He read the news from behind his anchor desk, solemn and concerned, giving the details of run-of-the-mill news stories on city council meetings, wrecks, fires, and news conferences. But often, Hill pursued larger stories. He had won several national awards for news-gathering, and two weeks after he met the young farmer, Hill was to fly to New York to receive yet another award, with a cash prize of $5,000. It was indeed a comfortable life, and Hill, who was married, had a substantial balance in his savings account, a nice home, a happy wife, and a faithful dog.

It was normal for a reporter, secure in his job, to pursue a lead like the one about Coolidge Conlee. He couldn't have known that just by doing his job, his life would become intertwined with an accused rapist and a shifty sheriff, that he would make a future president squirm, that he would help raise the slumbering forces of civil rights and progessive politics—and that he would live a drama that would endanger his life, rattle the foundations of polite Arkansas society, and ultimately shock the nation.

One

I run this county.

—Coolidge Conlee

On September 4, 1984, there was an ugly incident in Forrest City. It shook the proper white establishment, upset the musings at the Country Club, and left a cloud of fear hanging over the girls at Forrest City High School.

At two-thirty on a cloudy afternoon, a seventeen-year-old girl,* on her way home from school, stopped off at the run-down Diamond Burger near her house for a Coke, which she drank on her way home. An attractive young woman with shiny chestnut hair and a schoolgirl's trim figure, she was the daughter of a well-heeled and prominent funeral-

---

*To protect her identity, no reference to her name will be made.

home owner, who was a friend of the sheriff and a fraternity brother of the prosecutor. That afternoon she went into her family's fashionable house and plopped down on the floor in front of the television set. After just a few moments, she would say later, she heard a sound at the kitchen door, and then a thin white man came into the living room holding a paper sack in one hand and a gun in the other.

She said he forced her out to her car, pushed her down on the seat, and drove to a wooded area not far from where she lived. He took her out to a grassy field. He cut off her sweater and her bra with a pair of scissors he took out of the sack. Then he took off her blue jeans and panties and tried to have intercourse with her, but he stopped and told her she would have to help him. She said he made her perform oral sex on him, and after he ejaculated into her mouth, she spit out the semen. And for three seconds, she would say later, he entered her vagina, then pulled himself out without ejaculating again.

The man took the girl home, and forty-five days later, after identifying one man who turned out to have an airtight alibi, the young woman spotted a handyman named Wayne Dumond driving around grimy Forrest City in his pickup truck. She thought he was the man who had raped her, and she wrote down his license and turned him in.

After Dumond was arrested, the police brought the girl down to look at a lineup. She couldn't immediately pick him out from among the other blue-collared rednecks. Some said she was taken from the room by her father and the police chief.

When they returned, she fingered Wayne Dumond. And thus her story—and Wayne Dumond's—became a story of inexorable fate.

*   *   *

Mary Lou "Dusty" Wolf met Wayne in the neighborly church-going environment of rural Arkansas. It's where their story together began. Or did it? As Wayne might say, you shouldn't let the tail get ahead of the dog, or the dog'll chase the tail.

Maybe the story really began thirty years before in De-witt, Arkansas, where Wayne was born and raised and grew up on a farm. There, his mother died when he was seven years old, and his father remarried. Wayne and his brothers set out to make his stepmother's life miserable, and they did. Maybe it was then that Wayne grew into his hell-rais-ing ways. Maybe that's what would lead to a man's death in the army, and to drugs in Vietnam. Maybe the absence of a mother and a stern father ultimately led Dumond, with the gravelly, farmer's drawl and the wide steel eyes of the country, into the arms of an older, motherly woman like Dusty Wolf. Their courtship and settling down in Forrest City was certainly what led to Wayne's ultimate humili-ation. It was what ruined their lives. For had they not set-tled down in Forrest City, they never would have met Sher-iff Coolidge Conlee. And, just maybe, they never would have had to face the terror, and the horror, of helplessness against the power of the law.

Imagine a woman's flat voice, a distinctly Southern voice, quiet, reserved, yet full of strength and an indefatigable spirit. Imagine a voice that sometimes quavers, even when it's happy, a voice of a woman who's maintained her faith in the Lord even against impossible tests, a voice belonging to a woman of singular courage. That voice is Dusty Dumond's.

Imagine a woman with a pretty smile and an unobtrusive hairstyle, a woman who's older than her husband but somehow more innocent, a thin woman in glasses who's generous and loving toward her children. Imagine a woman who has fought for her family, who has written governors and presidents about her battles, who can't understand a criminal justice system that allowed the unthinkable. That woman is Dusty Dumond.

Dusty would later recount to Jack Hill how she and her daughter Jinger met Wayne and his three boys, and how she instantly liked him. When she brought Wayne's family a stew and chocolate pie, Wayne asked if he could return the serving dishes to her in person. Thus began a quick courtship that ended in May of 1983, with their marriage. They would soon settle in Forrest City. That was their first mistake.

As a result of his conversation with the young farmer, Jack Hill investigated Coolidge Conlee. One of the sheriff's renowned exploits was a highly publicized drug bust, in which Conlee supposedly rounded up a bunch of dealers and put them out of business. But there was more to the story than just Conlee's boasts about a big drug bust. And the more Hill looked into Conlee's doings, the more interesting the sheriff became. One of the first things he learned was Conlee's famous boast, "I run this county."

The sheriff, who came of age half a century earlier in the hot gambling heydays of Hot Springs, Arkansas, first rose to power as a school-board member favoring segregated schools. Everywhere he went he was followed by rumors that he enjoyed the fast life of chasing women and shooting craps. And truth be told, Conlee himself would say he loved to gamble. His partners called him Mr. C., but by the time he became Forrest City mayor and, later, sheriff of St. Francis

County, Conlee had found more respectability than the nickname might have indicated.

He didn't look like the redneck sheriff who fits the image of the rural south. There was no potbelly or jowls beneath a fleshy face. No giant of a man was this sheriff.

But Conlee could rival any of the sheriffs of Southern lore. He was a man of power and knew how to use it. It was no accident that his favorite phrase was, "I run this county."

When Coolidge Conlee was a young house gambler in the private, illegal casinos run in Hot Springs in the 1960s, he was allowed to play games by the grace of the imported gangsters and northern bootleggers who had moved to the quaint spa city a generation ago with piles of illegal cash. With nicknames like Sleepy and The Clay Pidgeon, the gangsters ran Hot Springs' bathhouses and gambling dens without fear of the law until another imported northerner— Winthrop Rockefeller—became governor and ordered a stop to it.

In Forrest City a couple of decades later, Conlee was again allowed to play without fear of legal retribution. Only this time his protector wasn't a northern bootlegger; it was a native Arkansan by the name of Gene Raff.

Raff was the silver-tongued and silver-haired elected prosecutor of the Delta's First Judicial District, a sprawling, nearly table-flat, six-county political division which included St. Francis County. Raff, whose ego was huge, did nothing to stop Conlee from operating as a lawless lawman. In fact, some attorneys later said the justice system did more than just allow Conlee to play; they said it encouraged him, just as Conlee had encouraged black St. Francis County honky-tonk owners to play; and, before that, Conlee himself had been encouraged by the bigshots to play in Hot Springs.

Coolidge acted like he was invulnerable against his critics; invulnerable against nosy reporters like that Jack Hill, the dull fellow from Channel 8; and invulnerable against his political enemies, like the County Judge, Carl Cisco. But the strangest things kept happening around Coolidge. His crop-dusting business, for instance, burned down; they were part of a failing business that had put Conlee several hundred thousand dollars in debt to the bank, which had loaned him the money. Hill might have been on a few trails, but Coolidge sure didn't seem nervous about it, because he didn't seem to think Hill could ever hurt him.

After Dusty and Wayne were married, Wayne's three boys and Dusty's girl lived in a modest clapboard house, tucked in a gulley on Barrow Hill Road in the middle of the woods atop Crowley's Ridge. To the side of the house was a little shed and nearby was a vegetable patch. The front yard sloped downward to the house, and a gravel driveway cut through the trees. There, on dark nights, a visitor unfamiliar with the surroundings could feel the isolation of the country and of the county. They had a phone, but in a real sense they were cut off from the outside world.

Wayne worked for a construction crew. For years he had taken odd jobs. Drivers who roll through Forrest City on I-40 can see the Holiday Inn where he worked as a maintenance man. He was also a good mechanic, farmer, and carpenter—in the days he worked. At night he liked his liquor; just as often as not it was whiskey and Coke.

November 1, 1984, was the Thursday before the election. In St. Francis County, incumbent Sheriff Conlee was running against Dave Parkman and another candidate.

Rumors had it that he was in a tight race.

November 1, 1984, was the day Wayne and Dusty got a knock on their door. Wayne was not wearing a shirt. Although fall had come, it was still warm in Arkansas. Wayne was holding his whiskey and Coke. He was amused to see the police standing in front of him. They demanded he come with them for questioning.

Later, Wayne would brag that he was still carrying his whiskey and Coke when he got into the back of the squad car.

> "Whatchyou got in that cup?" the police officer growled.
> "Coke."
> "Anything else?"
> "Naw."

Dumond would laugh about that moment. "Hey, I didn't know what was happening. I'm thinkin', this has gotta be a joke."

At the police station they lined him up. The jury never heard any evidence about the lineup, but Wayne would hear years later that a witness said the rape victim couldn't identify him until she was taken aside and told who to pick out. Wayne also claims he heard an officer open a door and yell to the people in the glassed-off i.d. room, "Take a good look at number two!"

Wayne, of course, was number two.

If that's true, why was he singled out?

Perhaps it was his past. In a sense, you might say it was his fate.

Wayne and his lawyers never could prove beyond all doubt that the lineup was tainted. But they did learn—after

Wayne's trial—that the victim had identified another man as her assailant, long before Wayne Dumond was picked up on the rape charge. Still another man, who was not identified, was brought in for questioning. These crucial pieces of evidence were never heard by the jury.

How was Wayne first identified? Call it bad luck. The victim was riding around Forrest City with a friend. At a stoplight, she said she glanced over at a man in a pickup truck. His crystal-blue eyes stuck out and struck her, she said. She told her friend, who wrote down the license number.

The driver was Dumond. No matter that his truck had a tailgate; the rapist's truck did not. No matter that the truck was the wrong color. That simple identification was just another in a chain of events that chained Dumond to the criminal justice system of St. Francis County.

By the next morning, it was on the radio that Dumond had been picked up for rape.

Jack Hill would later note that Conlee was running his campaign on the platform, "No unsolved crimes in the county." Now Conlee could brag he caught the rapist. No unsolved crimes in the county.

Four days later, Conlee handily won re-election.

Two

Let the people know the facts, and the country will be safe.

—Abraham Lincoln

A chill seemed to spread across the cluttered room as the fire inspector locked the door behind him. For the first time since beginning his investigation of Conlee, Hill sensed danger.

Hill had come to Forrest City to look at the fire department's report on a suspicious fire that a few months earlier had destroyed Conlee's crop-dusting business. But the fire inspector was not pleased. Hill was intruding. Public officials in the Delta weren't accustomed to having their files open to scrutiny.

Hill acted as if nothing were out of the ordinary. He

19

said little and began to take notes.

The first alarm was at 3:33 on a Saturday morning. Firemen responded, put out the blaze, and left the scene at 4:15. The second alarm came at 4:33. Sambo Hughes, Conlee's chief deputy, and a roustabout named Danny Burns, an auxiliary deputy and a local bail bondsman, had been at the scene of both fires. With them was an a crop-duster pilot named Ralph Brandon, who would later become a source for Hill.

In the report, the inspector concluded the fires were electrical in origin, and he was not suspicious of their cause.

Conlee told a local newspaper his loss totaled $700,000, including crop dusters and the hangar. He said the fire had been caused by a short in an adding machine cord, and that the blaze rekindled after firemen left. He would rebuild, he said; "Right now I'm waiting for the insurance adjustor to give the okay."

Hill didn't know much about fires, but he knew enough to see when things didn't add up. As he looked at his notes later, something leaped off the page. The time between fires. Eighteen minutes from the moment firemen left the scene to the moment of the report of the second fire. The second fire was a roaring inferno that could not be controlled before it gutted the business and destroyed three airplanes.

Eighteen minutes to destroy an airplane hangar, eighteen minutes from a waterlogged, under-control fire scene to a blazing hangar.

Some rekindling.

The fire inspector pushed a tape recorder toward Hill and snapped it on.

"All right, he snarled, "I want to know who's been going around saying I changed this report!"

Hill was taken aback. He had told the fire inspector over the phone that there had been rumors that the report had been doctored. It had been a ruse more than anything, a bit of psychology to get the inspector to turn over the document.

"Now, wait," Hill replied. "I don't know who said it originally. Someone said something to somebody, who passed it on to someone else, and finally I heard about it. I don't know where it got started. It's just talk out on the street."

Maybe it was seeing Hill so defensive that made the inspector back off. He let it rest.

Conlee didn't know it, but Jack Hill came prepared for him. Hill was the product of an idyllic childhood in the 1940s and '50s in the small, mountain town of Rogers in Northwest Arkansas. He was an only child to the salt of the earth. His father, Radus Hill, a decorated World War II veteran, worked at the Coca-Cola plant for nearly half a century, and was an usher at Central United Methodist Church for thirty years. His mother, Grace, was a lifetime schoolteacher and principal, and today there is a school named after her in Rogers. Throughout his childhood and young adulthood, Jack was known as the honest boy of Rogers. He never drank, and, after getting a mouthful of Ivory soap from his mother after cursing as a boy, never uttered another expletive. He was elected senior-high class president and voted most likely to succeed. When he took a job at the local radio station, most expected him to go far in the business.

The rock-solid values carried Jack through the crisis that would come later, and he always tried to live up to what others expected of him. He took it seriously when people said he was honest, hard-working, and obedient. Although such labels may be impossible always to live up to, Jack Hill tried. That was both his great triumph and his failing, as he took on the corrupt men of St. Francis County.

Jack's wife, Anne, was a product of Jackson, Mississippi, where she tried to live up to her family's tradition of prominence and success. Her father died when she was six weeks old, and she always looked up to her uncles as father figures. One of them was named president of the United States Chamber of Commerce.

Anne Campbell was quiet and shy, but very bright. She graduated easily at the top of her class at the private, exclusive Millsaps College in Jackson. Anne met Jack through a church group after Jack had taken a job with a Jackson television station.

After they married, they quickly settled into a comfortable life. It was exactly what Anne wanted—a happy home, a devoted husband, and a secure future. Anne trained for a career in bank management and excelled.

When Jack got a job offer in Jonesboro, Arkansas, he knew he wanted to return to his home state. He liked his job. On the streets of Jonesboro, people knew him and they tried to catch his eye. Anne took a job as a bank manager and became employee of the year.

They saved their money and Jack considered installing a swimming pool. But he never did, and it was a good thing. He didn't know it, but he was going to need the money that a pool would have cost him. For his security was about to be shattered.

From the beginning, Hill's investigation seemed to snowball. Investigative reporting can be a tricky business, with a bunch of dead ends and long hours amounting to nothing.

But from his first phone call (actually his second; his first call was a wrong number to the office of a local congressman), Hill scored. On that call, a former opponent of Conlee's, Bill Alexander, told Hill that he had gambled with Conlee, at least once at the sheriff's house. He also said he knew a man who had been selling drugs for the sheriff.

Alexander told Hill he could show him two or three places in the county that were home to high-stakes gambling games. He said he thought the sheriff got a cut of the takes; he told of $100,000 pots. And he added, almost as an afterthought: "It's higher than the sheriff."

Another source, whom Hill would vow to protect, told Hill about a game at a farmhouse, where Conlee showed up and went around shaking hands with the players, working the crowd like a politician.

"And the pots that day?" Hill asked.

"Tens of thousands."

The young man also told of bootlegging the night before an election, when booze was loaded from Conlee's liquor store into marked sheriff's cars, then transported to black neighborhoods. Hill made the inference that Conlee was trying to buy the black vote, a bloc he usually carried.

The young man made it clear he could not afford to be identified.

"I have to live with these people," he said. "And I know what they can do."

Three

I went from bein' a cocky schoolkid, to realizing that if there was any occupation I could do and do well it was bein' a soldier. I was a good soldier.

—Wayne Dumond

Wayne Dumond was born on September 10, 1949, in DeWitt, Arkansas, not too far from Elaine, the home of Arkansas' killing fields. Shortly after World War I, that dark farmland was the site of one of the worst race riots in U.S. history. Following rumors that black sharecroppers were to organize into a union, scores of blacks were hunted down and murdered. Yet the only persons to go on trial as a result of the massacre were blacks; they were convicted, but their cases gave rise to the NAACP, which rallied to their defense.

Wayne, a white boy, didn't have to worry too much about

25

the bigotry or the violence of the Delta. But the ignorance of the people in South Arkansas, their isolation, and yes, their pride, helped shape Dumond into the kind of man that would confuse manliness with forcefulness, patriotism with righteousness. Eventually, possessing few skills and a worldliness shaped by the Vietnam War, Dumond would have to flee his home to find a better way of life. It was more than coincidence that the same forces that shaped the nation and the world—Japanese economic power and the erosion of farm families—would define pivotal parts of Wayne Dumond's life. And in a real way, these forces led up to the horror and humiliation that awaited him.

Let's go back to Southeast Arkansas after the Second World War, when the nation was at peace and full of prosperity, and examine one boy's life. He was an unlikely boy to help realign Arkansas politics and influence the actions of a future U.S. president.

Wayne and his older brother resented their new Mom, who moved in and took over after their biological mother had died. Wayne grew up on a small thirty-acre farm, playing in the fields and in the livestock pond. He was always getting into trouble. He didn't try much in school. One time he torched the barn. He made it rough on his stepmother, and he got some whippings from his father in the bargain.

He kept asking God why He took his mother. He never did answer. She was thirty-nine.

So what happens to a boy who grows up in a Southern Baptist, Southern Arkansas household, under a quiet, strict father and a tough-minded stepmother?

He cuts class. He taunts a grade-school teacher, Miss Brewer, by calling her Miss Sewer. He drives her out of teaching after one year, the year Kennedy was killed. He doesn't care about much outside the fields of DeWitt. He spends his summers after adolescence working in the pea patches, picking peas, shelling peas, helping pull potatos, and harvesting corn. He builds fences. He chops wood. He rebuilds a '54 Chevrolet Impala his Dad bought for $35. He drops out of high school over the love of a DeWitt girl he took out in that car. And when he grows up and joins the military—a natural thing for a boy raised on patriotic principles in a town where the American flag graced front porches even when it wasn't Flag Day—his wild side takes over.

Wayne enlisted because he believed he would be drafted anyway. He wanted to get it out of the way before he started a life. In DeWitt he didn't think much about anti-war protests, draft dodging, draft-card burning. It was just a matter of course when he signed up for the army. It was 1967.

Dumond went into basic training at Fort Bliss, Texas. He was sent to Nam, where he spent a year in the infantry, first as a foreward observer, then as an artillery gunman. During his leave time, when he was back home in DeWitt, his old high school sweetheart jilted him and married another man. Until then he considered leaving the military, but after that he had nothing better to do but reenlist.

Mark it down. It was another decision that changed his life.

Later he would say that the military made him a better man. "I went from bein' a cocky schoolkid, to realizing that if there was any occupation I could do and do well it was bein' a soldier. I was a good soldier."

He was also a good drinker. It was not only socially acceptable to drink in the army, it was socially required. Dumond drank, and he drank heavily, something he hadn't done in DeWitt. It was also in the army, during Nam, that he started smoking pot. In the bush, he couldn't get alcohol; the ration was one hot beer a day. Though he could save the cans, it was tedious business, and the beer was always hot. Pot was quicker.

Dumond was like all the others who saw the horrors of Vietnam. He got shot at. He watched his friends carried off in body bags. But in a sense, he wasn't quite like the others: one day he became a hero.

On a mission in rugged Cambodia, his unit was preparing to give the go-ahead to nearby U.S. aircover to begin bombing. But Dumond, studying the map, suddenly realized that his people weren't where they thought they were. He told his captain, who at first didn't believe him, but then the captain agreed to ask the aircover to send smoke bombs, to see if Dumond was right.

The smoke bombs hit right on top of Wayne Dumond's unit. Had he not noticed the error, everyone probably would have been killed.

Dumond was decorated for his action. But it just didn't seem to be Dumond's fate to be a hero. Instead, when he returned to the States, his life took a turn for the worse. And nobody understood why he was always getting into trouble, why he wanted to take drugs and drink until he couldn't see straight.

Dumond had committed murder often, but nobody called it murder when he was wearing army green. In the Cambodian highlands one hot afternoon, he and his unit were hiking, hacking through the jungle, trying to avoid gunfire, slapping away mosquitoes, and cursing the humidity that clung to their skin. They came upon a village that wasn't on their maps. Someone remarked that they would have to "correct the map." But instead of doing that, the army boys decided just to wipe out the village.

> I'm goin' on R&R tomorrow. I'm goin' to Sydney, Australia. We just had a mad minute. We put several thousand rounds of ammunition in the village, killed everything in it. Then burned it. Walked off. I didn't count the bodies. Pigs, chickens, people. They were the enemy. But that was the sad thing about that war, you never knew who your enemy was.

He said it probably wasn't that different from My Lai.

But there was a key difference. Lt. William Calley got caught at My Lai, Dumond was to remark later. "But we didn't get caught."

Here's another irony in the life of Wayne Dumond. When he came back stateside, he realized Nam had messed him up. He started doing harder drugs. Hallucinogenics, like PCP and LSD, were favorites. He tripped often and hard, but he said he never had a bad trip because he had a strong enough mind to know he was tripping.

On one of his trips he saw a coffin. He approached it, scared. He remembered the seven-year-old boy standing at his mother's grave in a rural cemetery asking God why He took his mother. But this wasn't that trip. When he approached the coffin, he trembled. He moaned. He could not stop.

When he opened the coffin he found himself inside. It was Wayne Dumond, stretched out on the satin, observed by Wayne Dumond, redneck, farmer, mechanic, patriot, soldier, drug-addict.

It was a wonderful life.

* * *

Wayne's alibi was that he was home sick the day of the rape. His family swore he had a bad fever. A seventeen-year-old boy they had sort of adopted for the summer would swear that he saw Wayne in the house all afternoon.

Wayne's boss really didn't know where he was that day, he claimed. On a construction crew it was hard to keep track of everyone's comings and goings.

Prosecutors would try to tear apart his alibi. Only those who had a stake in helping Wayne were willing to help him, it seemed.

Dusty, ever the fighter, would not take the rape charge lying down. She wrote the newspapers. She wrote the rape victim's family. She even phoned the victim—a rather audacious act, if one considers that she was the accused rapist's wife talking directly to his supposed victim. But Dusty was that kind of woman. She was always a tremendous ally in a fight.

In her letter to her family, she would recall later in court testimony:

> I explained to them all the details of why it couldn't have been him, where we were, the circumstances. I wanted the rapist caught if there was one out there. They were leaving my family defenseless—my daughter and I—if there was a rapist out there, by taking the wrong man. And I gave them—I gave away every bit of our alibi that day of circumstances. I told them everything. I even sent them a picture of our family—our loving family. They had a picture.

Of course, Wayne was in that picture, and his eyes were in that picture. It would be his eyes—the victim would swear it—it was his eyes she could never forget.

Dusty hand-carried the letter to the funeral home.

The Dumonds really didn't know what they were up against. The victim's father was a fraternity brother to the assistant prosecutor, who was the sheriff's private attorney. The victim's father was the coroner.

And the rape victim's cousin was the governor of Arkansas, Bill Clinton. Some said that as a political favor, Clinton had appointed the chief prosecutor, Gene Raff, to the Arkansas Police Commission. Raff's trusted deputy, Fletcher Long, was to lead the prosecution of Dumond. Clinton, of course, would parlay his Arkansas power base into the presidency. Is it any wonder that a redneck like Wayne Dumond and his naive wife were about to be knocked over like a pair of bowling pins? Is it really any wonder they never had a chance at justice?

The day after Wayne's arrest, Wayne's bond was set at $100,000; then it was lowered to $75,000. The Dumonds had to come up with 10 percent of it in cash, and back the rest. That was going to take time.

Wayne and Dusty were apart for two weeks. With the help of Wayne's father, they scraped the bond money together. They found a bondsman out of Little Rock who backed it up, and they got Wayne out of jail. To his family it was a big relief, but they should have left him in jail.

Four

The only security of all is a free press. . . . The agitation
it produces must be submitted to. It is necessary to keep
the waters pure.

—Thomas Jefferson

Time marched on in the Delta as Jack continued to probe,
prod, poke, procure. He had talked to more than two hundred people. Most had heard of Conlee's shenanigans. But
none of the sources was more valuable than the Arkansas
State Police's file on Coolidge Conlee, which Hill heard about
through contacts and then requested to see under the Freedom of Information Act. At more than an inch thick, the
file recounted Conlee's past in Hot Springs gambling houses
and told of apparent instances in which Conlee allowed drugs
to be sold for the sheriff's office. Hill spent a late night and

early morning at Channel 8 in the small newsroom, going over the file. Over his head, mice scurried above the ceiling.

The file was damning. One informant told the State Police he was selling marijuana for Conlee and deputy Larry Henley. After the informant was wired by the State Police, he told Conlee, "I've got you some money that I owe you. There it is, $340. That's, you know, for the dope and stuff. And I've got in with some guys in West Memphis now. They will come over here to my territory if you still want to do it."

"Well, what do they want to deal?" Conlee asked.

On another occasion, the informant met with Henley. He gave Henley $50 he supposedly had collected for selling pot. The pot came from the sheriff's office, but Henley hadn't sold it like he said. He really turned it over to the State Police.

"Have you got anything else I can get?" the informant asked. "I have another one sold if I can get it."

Henley said, "Okay . . . look at this. Is this what you wanted? No I can't do this . . . that hasn't been to court yet," he said in reference to a bag of marijuana taken from an evidence drawer. Henley then got a second bag from the drawer. "There ought to be several dollars worth there," Henley said.

Nowhere in the State Police transcripts was there any indication that Conlee and Henley were trying to make drug arrests through the informant. He was simply selling the drugs and turning the money over to the sheriff's office.

The State Police evidence dated from 1981, shortly after Conlee took office.

So why wasn't he prosecuted?

Simply put, it was because local prosecutors wouldn't

charge him. Deputy prosecutor Fletcher Long, who would also serve as Conlee's personal attorney, said the State Police investigation simply revealed an unethical investigatory procedure, not criminal activity. Circuit Judge John Anderson wrote Prosecutor Gene Raff, "It is the opinion of the court that your office would not be justified in taking any further action based on the [State Police] report and that the evidence presented to me does not justify me in calling a Grand Jury to consider the matter."

There was only one thing wrong with Anderson's logic. In Arkansas, a circuit judge usually had no role in determining whether a grand jury is called. The normal procedure is for the prosecutor to call a grand jury; the judge simply empanels it.

But either way, a grand jury wasn't going to be called on Conlee. Raff had made it clear he wasn't going to do it. And Judge Anderson, a federal case would reveal later, was strongly influenced by Raff.

It was cut and dried. At the bottom of the file, Hill noticed the State Police investigator's comment that the case would be closed because Raff wouldn't prosecute.

The evidence was overwhelming to Hill. Not only was Conlee an outlaw lawman, but he was being protected by the system in which he operated.

Dumond's family kept pinning their hopes on the alibi, this skinny kid named Robert Hughes, who got stranded in Forrest City after his family went to Arizona without him. He was seventeen. Dumond and Dusty got to know him through their church, and Dumond told Dusty they should keep the boy in the shed near their house. No, she said, he would live with the boys, in the house.

On September 11, 1984, the day the funeral-home owner's daughter claimed she was abducted and raped, summer was still lingering, adding to Wayne's fever. Wayne picked that day to be sick. His friends would reflect later: some people win the lottery, Dumond destroys his only alibi with the flu.

He went into work the morning of the rape. But his upset stomach prevented him from returning that afternoon.

Robert Hughes would vouch for Dumond's illness. He was at home when Dumond was home sick that afternoon. He said Dumond never left. But Robert Hughes's word wasn't good enough to the criminal justice system of St. Francis County.

Dumond said he kept to himself pretty much at work that morning. "I don't like to complain about bein' sick. It's just not manly. 'I don't feel very good.' But I will today. I wish I had then."

Hughes did use Wayne's pickup that day. But that didn't make him a suspect because the victim identified the wrong kind of pickup.

On October 28, Wayne was again in the wrong place at the wrong time. His boy had a wart on him. Dumond took him in to have it burned off. While they were riding back from the doctor's office in the pickup, the victim picked out Dumond as her assailant. She spotted him at a traffic light.

When they finally picked him up, Dumond was half drunk and watching "20/20," the same program he would become a star of a few years later.

Dumond likes to brag about drinking that drink in the back of the squad car, even as he was being hauled in for rape. After he was identified in the lineup he said was phony, they threw him in the drunk tank for three hours. Then they transported him to the county jail, where he spent thirteen days.

His life out on bond was a dog's life. Dusty was off work because of foot problems, and drew only a small amount of worker's comp pay. With the rape charge hanging over his head, Dumond couldn't hold a steady job.

One day he and Dusty saw an ad in the newspaper for "assembly work." They responded, and the next thing they knew, they put down a $60 deposit to buy materials to make handmade dolls. A Florida company ran the business, and they bought everything the Dumonds and other down-on-their-luck manufacturers across the country produced. Dumond spent his days at home making knitted clowns and other doll figures. He made six dollars a doll, and could make ten a day. So the Dumonds were able to scrape by through doll money, disability, and unemployment checks.

The dolls would serve him well later. In prison he had plenty of time to make little dolls.

Dusty, on her crusade, wrote a letter to the Wynne, Ark., *Progress*, calling for justice, and pointing out that she doubted most of the news media would bother to investigate Coolidge Conlee. A reporter would later point out the verbal attack on Conlee was followed by a sick retribution against Dumond.

That Wednesday night, March 6, at their new church, Second Baptist in Forrest City, an encouraged Dusty stood up and gave testimony. She said that her husband was doing well, that they had spiritual strength despite their adversity, that Wayne was out of a job but with the Lord, that they felt confident they would win his case. She asked for their prayers, She explained that he did nothing all day but make dolls, and that he would again be at home the next day without much purpose.

Dumond would wonder about this later. The members of the church prayed for the Dumonds. But he couldn't help but reflect that someone in the church knew his exact schedule the next morning. Then he realized he was just looking for something suspicious when there probably was nothing there.

That Second Baptist service was on Wednesday, March 6, 1985. The next day would be the worst of their lives.

Five

We believe in public enlightenment as the forerunner of justice.

—Code of Ethics, Society of Professional Journalists

Ralph Brandon belonged to the adventurous breed of agriculture pilots, those low-flying, daredevil crop-dusters whose seat-of-the-pants legacy gave rise to thrilling stunts at air shows. He was also the kind who could not be manipulated by the justice system of St. Francis County, because he lived somewhere else. That and his happenstance proximity to Coolidge Conlee's burned crop-dusting business made him an ideal source for Jack Hill. It was logical for Hill to talk to Brandon—the pilot was listed as one of three people at the site of the fires the night they happened, and he was the only one of the three who wasn't beholden to Conlee.

The night of the fires, Brandon told Hill, his trailer was parked near Conlee's hangar so he could spend the night in it before a dawn crop-dusting job. He was awakened by a car horn. A passerby had spotted the first fire, and both of them had put the fire out before firemen arrived.

When they left, there was no danger, he said.

"The next thing I knew Danny Burns and Sambo Hughes were yelling for me to get out," Brandon said. "I opened my eyes, and it looked like the whole world was on fire!"

Brandon said Forrest City Aviation had been in financial trouble and wasn't well run.

Looking back, he thought it was strange that a second blaze could break out in less than thirty minutes. He also thought it was strange that the guard dogs had been moved and were not at the hangar the night of the fires.

Another source, mechanic Bruce Hayes, told Hill he had been installing a new engine in a plane when he was told emphatically by the sheriff that the plane had to be out of the hangar by Thursday night. Hayes said the sheriff told him he did not want to be liable in case of a fire.

The Forrest City Aviation fire would serve him well in his planned reports on Conlee, but Hill didn't stop there. He also got color on the sheriff, including a tale from State Police trooper Jim Lester, who was working undercover in 1969 at the Hot Springs' Ohio Club, an illegal gaming casino. When State Police raided the club, Conlee tried to hide behind a couch in the dice room, Lester told Hill.

"What are you doing here?" an officer demanded of Conlee.

"Well, I was just trying to get some sleep," Conlee said.

"He's trying to get some sleep, nothing!" Lester snorted. "He's the pit boss!"

*   *   *

There was one small detail that hovered over Jack Hill as he continued his investigation. The television station he worked for was sold to Channel Communications, a Nashville firm who bought it from the Arkansas Hernreichs. Although the new owners pledged to continue KAIT's reputation for thoughtful, thorough reporting, Hill couldn't help but wonder. Not long after Channel Communications took over, one of the first moves was to cut the 6 P.M. nightly newscast from an hour to half an hour.

Reporter Michael Kelley of *The Commercial Appeal*, Memphis's daily newspaper, interviewed Hill about the new ownership. It was a story because KAIT had developed a national reputation for news, and its dominance of its time slot was unheard of. It was the highest-rated program of any kind in the nation, capturing about 80 percent of viewers. But Kelley picked up on the notion that new ownership might mean changes, and he noted the half-hour cut in the nightly news.

"If there are many more cutbacks," he concluded in *The Commercial Appeal* article, "Northeast Arkansas may lose its unique status in the television community—a little place where big ideas grow."

After Wayne got out of the service, his father gave him an acre of ground in DeWitt, right next to the old man's ranch. Wayne built himself a house in 1978, shortly after his brother drowned while coon hunting. He and his wife settled in there with their three boys, Dale, Michael, and Joey, and lived there for four or five years. Dumond had a normal life, though he had those army secrets, the secrets of drugs and killing.

He ran the parts department for a big manufacturing company in DeWitt. He had the lead role in the First Assembly of God's Christmas play for three straight years. It was a Scrooge-like character, an old man.

He had received a minor role the first year. But the leading player was a slouch. Dumond told the director, "If that ol' boy don't wanna do it, I'll do it."

"Are you sure you can do it?"

"Yeah, I can do it."

Dumond chuckled about it later. "People said, 'That's Wayne Dumond? That's that shy little ol' boy?' "

At this point in his life, Dumond likes to say, "I was good people. I had a good job, nice home, went to church."

Of course, he was still a heavy drinker and a heavy pot user. In fact, he grew his own weed. He set up lights and fertilized soil in his cellar. He pinched the buds and let them dry. But it was for his own use, he said. He might have given some away, but he didn't sell it.

Dumond established a routine. He worked hard in the mornings; then at lunch he would roll a joint, smoke it, come back to work, and take it easy. But he got the job done, and nobody had any complaints.

In late 1980, he and his wife began to split, and they were divorced by the spring of 1982. At first Dumond was to get only the two youngest boys, but eventually all three of them were handed over to him in the settlement.

By 1982, the Reaganomics farm recession was hitting hard in states like Arkansas. Towns like DeWitt were drying up. With the farms went the implement dealers, the coffee shops, the hardware stores, the gas stations. The multimillion-dollar manufacturing company where Dumond headed the parts department shut down, and Dumond was laid off.

He scouted around for a job. What lured Dumond to Forrest City was the Sanyo plant, recruited by the same Chamber of Commerce that called the town "a big little city in the USA." With the help of Governor Bill Clinton, Forrest City had scored a coup by winning Japanese investment. Forrest City had been hit hard by the recession, but the Sanyo plant—where they made color television sets—was a crown jewel in Clinton's economic development program.

It's more than a little ironic that Dumond—a fan of Reagan—was driven from his home by the Reagan recession to the town and county that had scored big from Japanese investment. At the time, though, it just seemed like the place to go. It was still in the Delta, his home region, and it was still in his home state.

But Dumond never worked at Sanyo. Travelers of Interstate 40 are familiar with his job locale. It was the Holiday Inn right by the interstate. Dumond worked in maintenance. He helped redecorate the whole hotel.

> I was workin' there, makin' decent money. Me and the kids rented a little ol' house out in the country, we was livin' out there, they was goin' to school. We were all real happy, we were gettin' along. They were good kids. They still are good kids. And then Dusty came into our lives.

Dusty was in the middle of a divorce when she cooked up that stew. Dumond, introduced to her through a mutual friend, was bowled over. He saw her at a 1982 Christmas party. Wayne brought some of the corn whiskey that he would make on his stove. It was crystal clear and the hit of the party. But for Wayne, the hit was Dusty.

It was a whirlwind courtship. We married in May (after meeting in March). The chemistry was right. Around her I felt so at ease. But yet—she was, I don't know how to describe it.

To Wayne, Dusty was high society. "She was a lady. She was adventurous, smart. Very intelligent."

She knew about his past. They didn't talk about it much, though it was there to be discussed if they wished. But it wasn't his youthful mistakes that she saw when she looked at him. She saw the good in him.

One day Dumond quit Holiday Inn. He was asked to do some welding with what he considered inferior equipment. He threw down the welder in disgust and said he was going to find a better job. He said it was the sorriest move he ever made.

Dumond was hired by a one-eyed man who owned a construction company, with a specialization in putting in septic systems. Dumond, ever the handyman, did everything from tightening bolts to heavy lifting.

He knew later he never should have quit the Holiday Inn. His alibi was destroyed by the fact that he worked at a place that didn't really keep track of where their workers were.

No alibi? In Forrest City, if you're accused of raping the wrong girl, you'd better have one.

As the leaves began to turn and Dumond faced the rape charge, Hill began shooting in earnest for the Conlee series. Conlee and his people knew what was coming. The Forrest City newspaper printed a letter complimenting Conlee for doing "such a fine job," despite the "slanderous remarks" of critics.

The letter went on, "I know it must be hard to ignore the way these people call a nearby television station to give rumors and a scoop to an ambitious reporter who has dreams of creating 'the story of the year.' "

It was signed, "Dealing in facts not fiction, I've known him for 33 years—his wife, Mrs. Coolidge Conlee."

In the fall campaign, Conlee ran against what he called the slander of Channel 8. Hill became a campaign issue. In ads in local newspapers, Conlee tried to counteract the "lies" of Channel 8 with a list of claims under a giant head-line: THE TRUTH. Under eleven headings of "Truth," Con-lee outlined his qualifications for re-election. For Hill, one item stood out above all the others in the ad: "Truth: no major unsolved crimes in St. Francis County" since Conlee took over as sheriff.

At home while Jack was working, Anne dreaded the phone calls. When she answered a gruff voice growled: "We know where you live. We know where you work. We know your comings and goings. And if you're smart, you'll get your husband off this thing."

Terrified, she hung up. But she thought she had to be a good soldier. She said nothing to Jack. The series had to go on.

Hill planned to air the Conlee series for the November "sweeps"—a major ratings period on which ad costs are based. Ten reports, airing at 6 P.M. and 10 P.M. for five days, were to deal with Conlee's background, his gambling, his hiding behind the couch at the Ohio Club. Then Hill would follow with the 1981 investigation involving the sale of mari-juana through the sheriff's office, the sheriff's connection with bootlegging, Conlee's manipulation of the black vote, and the fires at Forrest City Aviation. Hill would also mention lawsuits against Conlee and deputies by prisoners accusing officers of abuse. The claims totaled $1.5 million.

Station manager Darrell Cunningham urged caution. Aware of the new ownership, he said attorneys would have to review the material.

On a bright November morning, in a conference call, Cunningham asked attorney Jon Ross if he had any problems with Hill's scripts that had been sent to him.

"I certainly dooooooo!" came the reply. He ripped apart Hill's work. Hill suggested too much about other public officials who were protecting Conlee, Ross said. He had doubts about the evidence of arson at Forrest City Aviation. He even questioned if such a small station should be involved in such an extensive investigation in the first place. Such a story, he said, would be better left to "20/20" or "60 Minutes."

Hill was stung by Ross's critique. The scripts would have to be reworked. November sweeps came and went, and the series was put on hold.

Eventually, though, he saw that Ross made some good points. He used the criticisms to make his work stronger. He dug deeper. He found suppliers to Forrest City Aviation who said Conlee owed them money, cementing opinions that the business had been in financial trouble. Hill also learned that a night or two before the fires, Conlee's chief deputy, Sambo Hughes, bought eight containers of lighter fluid from a Forrest City convenience store. How'd he find that out? He'd heard rumors to that effect, so he asked the store clerk, and she told him.

The mild Southern winter brought Hill closer to his goal.

By mid-January, Hill thought he was ready. But there would be no conference call this time. He brought his scripts, supporting documents, and videotapes to a meeting with Nashville attorney Aubrey Harwell, who worked closely with Channel Communications. The courtly Harwell, a Southern gentleman, listened closely to Hill's presentation as Ross sat in. Hill had prepared for the meeting as if for an examination. He had documents on hand. The attorneys were impressed.

"Son of a bitch!" exclaimed Ross while reading the State Police file on Conlee.

"Who's the local prosecutor?" they asked. "Who's the U.S. attorney? Why don't they do something?"

"I don't know," Hill said. But he still had his suspicions that Conlee was being protected by the system.

Darkness fell and the meeting ended. Few changes were made in the scripts.

Monday. February 11, 1985. It was time.

Hill settled into the anchor's chair to read the 6 o'clock newscast. The lead story was the first of ten reports on Coolidge Conlee. The series had been well-publicized through a KAIT promotional blitz. A quarter-page ad had appeared that afternoon in the Forrest City *Times-Herald*. Hill knew there was going to be a big audience in St. Francis County.

The pumping news theme rolled. The cameraman yelled, "Stand by!" The camera's red light came on, and Hill started to read. He stumbled, caught himself, then forged ahead. Later, he remarked to weatherman Terry Wood that a distraction had caused him to fumble.

No, Wood said. it was nervousness. He was right.

The response to the reports was overwhelming and immediate. Mrs. Coolidge Conlee wrote to the newspaper again.

She said, "I have watched with disgust. There were several discrepancies in both reports." But others praised Hill. One St. Francis County resident thanked him personally for exposing the county's leadership.

He also got a letter from another Forrest City resident:

"I am writing in response to the letter that Mrs. Conlee wrote to you. She stood by her man, and I feel I have the same right." She explained that her husband had been unjustly accused of rape. It was signed by Dusty Dumond. Hill had never heard of her or Wayne. He filed the letter away.

By the end of the week-long blitz of news reports, Conlee had become the talk of Northeast Arkansas. KAIT ran a full-page ad announcing all of Hill's reports would be condensed into a half-hour program, to run that Sunday. The show would be called, "I Run This County." There was no mistaking who it would be about.

Hill ended his series with a stand-up, facing the camera. He was beside the mailbox at the gutted Forrest City Aviation building as he read his lines:

> Conlee likes to say that since he's been elected sheriff, there is not a single major unsolved crime in St. Francis County. But the evidence would seem to indicate there is at least the question of one major unsolved crime in the county. And it involves the sheriff's own business. For Region 8 News, this is Jack Hill reporting.

Finally it was over. But it really had just begun. Jack and Anne's lives would never be the same again.

Six

Then my whole world fell apart.

—Wayne Dumond

Their faces were distorted by nylon stocking masks. One had a pistol, the other a knife. They wore thin, bluish-green surgical gloves to keep the blood off their hands.

As they approached the Dumond's rural frame house outside Forrest City, Wayne sat inside, drinking and watching soap operas. Beside him the half-gallon bottle of Jim Beam whiskey was two-thirds empty. His guns were hung on the back wall. He didn't hear the popping of gravel under car tires as the masked men drove down his driveway.

It was early afternoon on that cold, sunny March 7, 1985. Dumond, taking another drink of whiskey, cursed his bad luck. He had been unable to find a new job since being fired

49

in the fall from work as a mechanic and handyman, and now nobody wanted to hire him because of what that girl had said about him. But deep down Dumond never thought he would go to trial on the rape charge. He figured the girl had just been confused or frightened when she identified him.

It had started off a routine day. I was helping Larry Taylor on the side. That morning I spent up there sanding cabinets, putting sealer in cabinets, and I did that until about lunch time. I had it in my mind that I was gonna go to the lumber yard to get some more materials. I went home. I watched some TV. I watched the news. Jack Hill. Channel 8.

Dumond was joking about watching Hill. That wouldn't come until later.

He also had plans that day to use a tractor he had borrowed from a neighbor to plow some nearby ground; Dumond wanted to plant a few rows.

Sometime in the early afternoon, I walked to the mailbox. I walked the piece of ground I was gonna plow just to see what the moisture was like. I went through the mail to see what was there. Bills, you know, a check or two for some dolls.

He was restless. He got up from the couch and went into the small kitchen. Dumond did a lot of housework because he was home so much. As he was putting away some clean dishes left on the counter, he heard the sound of the unlocked front door banging open.

He turned and saw the masked men barging in. Dumond stumbled toward his guns, but he was stopped by the sound of a cocking pistol.

"Then my whole world fell apart."

They wrestled him to the floor just off the kitchen, in the dinette area. The shorter man was chattering crazily, but Dumond couldn't hear any of the words. All he could think of was the cocked pistol pressing against his temple.

> They bind my hands behind me. . . . I'm terrified. I don't know what's happenin', I don't know why it's happenin', I don't know what these people are gonna do or nothin'. This pistol's stuck to my head; the hammer's back because I heard him cock it. And there's nothing more dangerous in the world than a cocked pistol.

They rolled him on his left side, pulled out a ball of white cotton twine, and fastened his hands, already tied together, to his feet. On the farms of Arkansas, they would have said he was hog-tied. He was completely helpless.

The men unzipped Dumond's blue jeans, then slid them down around his knees. Without a word, the taller man pulled out a straight surgical knife—and began to cut into his scrotum.

He begged and pleaded and screamed.

"Why me? What are you doing, man? Why? Goddamn! Aaah!"

But it was as if they didn't hear. The shorter man calmly held the pistol to Wayne's head while the other man worked quickly, efficiently, to open Dumond's scrotum, and with a spurt of blood, the testicles slipped out and slid into the widening red pool on the linoleum floor.

"I have been in pain in my life but nothing like that. Never. Nothing hurt like that before or since."

Dumond, dizzy with pain, thought he heard the short man congratulate the taller man for a job well done.

"Yeah," said the second man. "Mr. C. would be proud."

Then they left him to bleed to death from his crotch.

Dumond, weak from blood loss, dazed, and still helplessly tied up, alternately yelled for help, tried to free himself, and then daydreamed as he slipped in and out of consciousness. For two hours he lay there, bleeding, praying, squeezing his legs together to slow the flow of blood.

> I'm cryin', "Oh God, what's happened? Shit!" I'm bleedin', I know I'm bleedin'. I'm tied up. I'm trying to squeeze my legs together . . . and I'm starting to get real weak and I passed out. I was aware, though, when the kids came home. That was the point I had to make it to. I knew they'd be there a quarter to four. And they did.

Joey, nine, and Michael, eleven, were laughing as they walked down the driveway. Barely conscious, with two-thirds of his blood gone and perhaps twenty minutes to live, Dumond came to himself and heard them coming. He knew his young sons would see him this way—and perhaps never be the same again.

The youngest son took one look at the bloody mess, and he yelled, "Oh, no!" and shot back out the door.

> I thought, "Oh, no, my help's run off." But the oldest one stayed with me. He says, "Daddy, what happened?" I says "Get a knife, get me loose, right now, and I'll tell you." And he did, he stepped over me to get to a drawer and got a paring knife and cut all the string.

Wayne got it in his head to call his lawyer, Larry Horton, and he tried to crawl into the next room.

A few seconds later, Mr. McCain, Dumond's neighbor, alerted by Joey, came running in to see Dumond lying there, too weak to move, surrounded by cut string and a metallic-smelling pool of blood.

Michael sat in a kitchen chair. He was staring, as if in a trance, at his blood-stained hands.

McCain cast his gaze back toward the kitchen. In the middle of the floor, amid the bright blood and cut twine, were two other objects. He knew what they were from his days growing up on a farm, when he'd seen hogs castrated. But this time he realized that the bloody, misshapen severed testicles belonged to Wayne Dumond.

Dusty was at the chiropractor's office in town. She put in a full day at work that day at the Sanyo plant, the company that Bill Clinton, when he recruited it, touted as an economic savior for East Arkansas. At 4 o'clock, when she got off work, she met Jinger at the chiropractor's office so she could give her daughter a ride home. While Dusty was there with her daughter, she got a call that there was an emergency, that she was needed at home immediately. The chiropractor told her to leave Jinger, that he would give her a ride home, so Dusty left her there. She got in her car and began driving as fast as she could.

Her mind raced. She kept wondering if maybe one of the boys was hurt. And there was a tractor at home; she wondered if Wayne had gotten hurt on the tractor. When she got home she could see the boys at the end of the neighbors' driveway, so she knew they were all right.

But then she saw the ambulance, and she knew something was terribly wrong.

The neighbors, the McCains, were outside when Dusty got there, and they held her back from the house. They wouldn't let her go in, they said he'd lost a lot of blood, and they forced her to stay outside. Here's how she would tell it in court:

> When they told me that he'd been wounded so badly that they didn't think he would live, I told them I . . . I said, "How has he been wounded? Did he hurt himself or was— did someone hurt him?" And they said, "Well, he didn't do it to himself."

And Dusty, struggling against them, said, "If he has only two minutes to live, I want to be with him."

She tore herself away and walked into the horror. The blood was all over the kitchen floor, and in the laundry room, and there was so much of it, it made her head spin and it hypnotized her, and she couldn't see anything in the blood; it held her spellbound.

Then she saw what looked like intestines in the middle of the blood.

> It was sections of bluish . . . and I thought that they'd cut his guts out. I didn't know what they'd done to him. I could see on—his lower extremities was exposed to me and he was just nothing but blood.

It took her a few moments to realize that what she had thought were her husband's intestines was really the twine that was used to tie him up. Coated with blood, the strips of twine looked blue and sectioned. But when she saw his scrotum she still didn't fully realize what had happened.

The paramedics snipped Wayne's pants off him and zipped him into a shock suit. They pumped the suit up to apply pressure to the wound, and the pain shot through him. They asked Dusty how tall he was, how much he weighed, how old he was. She was responding without thinking, still hypnotized by the blood.

In downtown Forrest City, Sheriff Conlee was in his courthouse office when he heard on the sheriff's scanner a call of alarm from Deputy Bennie Brewer.

"A man's down," Brewer's voice crackled across the scanner. There was panic in his voice, and Conlee sat up and took notice. "There's blood everywhere. Send somebody out here."

Conlee, a thin, wiry, nervous chain-smoker, immediately headed out to Dumond's house. When he arrived, the sheriff met an ambulance in the narrow road, its red lights flashing.

Dusty would testify that she got in the car to go with Wayne to the hospital, then saw Conlee approaching.

> And I stopped the car and I stood beside the car with the door open and I said, "Don't go in there. The paramedics are coming out. They need the road." And it's just a one-lane road.

Conlee ignored her and drove around her, momentarily blocking the ambulance.

The sheriff was agitated as he walked into the Dumond home, and he complained loudly of not being able to locate it easily. He walked through the rooms quickly, and in the back bedroom, Conlee picked up a billfold. In it he found Dumond's identification, and he recognized the name of the accused rapist. After picking up the blood-soaked cut twine and Dumond's whiskey bottle, Conlee went to the hospital and heard the details of Dumond's castration.

Dusty would recall later in court:

> The family doctor . . . came into me and he said, "Well, Dusty, where has he been hurt? How has he been hurt? Has he been shot? Has he been knifed or whatever?"
>
> And Sheriff Conlee came in with some deputies behind him and he said, "Well, he's been castrated." He told the doctor.

Wayne would later tell her about the "Mr. C." comment. Both of them knew who Mr. C. was—Mr. Cool, Coolidge Conlee.

From the hospital, Conlee called State Police Lieutenant Phil Osterman and arranged to take Osterman back out to the Dumonds'. A quiet, hardworking veteran of the State Police, Osterman was appalled by the story of the castration. He readily agreed to go with Conlee.

When the two officers arrived at the house, it soon became apparent to Osterman that Conlee was obsessed with the testicles that were still on the kitchen floor in the middle of the drying blood.

"I'm gonna take these for evidence," Conlee told the lieutenant.

He found a matchbox and a pair of tweezers on a nearby table, then walked toward the testicles, leaving his footprints in the sticky blood. He stooped to pick up the testicles, grasping one with the tweezers, and looked at the soft tissue. The sheriff looked fascinated, Osterman thought, even spellbound. Conlee put the testicle in the open matchbox and picked up the other one.

"Why are you doing this?" Osterman asked him.

He was already annoyed that the crime scene had been left unattended while Conlee had gone to the hospital, and he was amazed at the sheriff's weird obsession with the body parts.

"Well, I need these for evidence," Conlee said. "They're evidence."

The record isn't clear on where Conlee went next, but at some point he transferred the testicles from the matchbox to an empty quart jar and went to the funeral home owned by the father of the rape victim. Conlee poured clear formaldehyde—normally used on corpses at the funeral home— over the testicles. He wanted to preserve them.

Across town, the rape victim's father was summoned from his regular steak dinner by the sheriff. He arrived at his funeral home to find Conlee with the jar containing the testicles of the man accused of raping his daughter.

Together they rode back to dinner, the jar behind them in the sheriff's car.

Seven

Television must stand up for the Bill of Rights, not fall down. The First Amendment is a mandate, not a suggestion.

—Edward R. Murrow

The bleeding had stopped, but he needed immediate surgery. They would airlift him to Memphis.

Almost immediately, Conlee began telling acquaintances that Wayne had castrated himself. Later that rumor would be like salt on his wound, but for now Wayne had to deal with another kind of hurt.

The pain really started in Memphis. The doctors were squeezing where they cut him to stop the bleeding.

"God, please," he begged them. He was strapped down. "Oh, God. Oh, God! Either quit, gimme something for the pain, or kill me!"

59

Finally they knocked him out. When he awoke, he was sewn up. He stayed in the hospital for six days, but the pain would take years to go away. For a long time, the most painful thing he did was have a bowel movement. He could barely walk; he couldn't bear to sit down.

At first Wayne didn't want it in the newspaper. He was ashamed. But there was no way to fight the publicity. He made big headlines two days later, when the news of the horror finally filtered through. Dumond's shame hurt nearly as bad as his wound. He decided to supress the incident. He wouldn't think about it. And he would not talk about everything that happened to him on that day. Not for a long time would he tell it all.

When Wayne was released, he began the slow process of rehabilitation. He was mad and scared. To this day he has no scrotum. It is simply a flat piece of skin where his testicles were. But he didn't think of himself as less of a man. If anything, it was kind of like the things that happened to him in the army. It made him more of a man. It made him know what he could endure.

With the help of hormone injections, Dumond could still get an erection. He could still be a complete husband to Dusty. After a while, he carefully made love to her. It hurt him like hell.

For Jack Hill, the castration was another example of the horrors of St. Francis County.

The 10 P.M. newscast on that Thursday had been routine. He took a few phone calls after he went off the air. But then he got another phone call. This one was different. A shaky woman's voice said: "I can't tell you who I am. But a man was castrated today near Forrest City. You may have heard of him. His name is Wayne Dumond. He's been charged with rape and was awaiting trial. I just thought you'd want to know."

One of the first things that crossed Hill's mind was that the castration might involve the sheriff. A second thing that crossed his mind was that he, Jack Hill, could be to blame. His reports on St. Francis County, maybe, had somehow caused the few power-mad men to reassert their dominance.

Dumond. The name did ring a bell. He went to his filing drawer and began fishing through the letters he'd received following his series of reports on St. Francis County. Sure enough, there, in the stack of them, was the letter from Dusty Dumond.

Hill couldn't confirm the castration story that night. Not surprisingly, no one in the St. Francis County Sheriff's Office would talk to him. By the following afternoon, all they had was the basics. KAIT ran a brief "reader" (no video) on the Friday 6 P.M. newscast.

But by Saturday, the newspapers had jumped on the story, and *The Commercial Appeal,* the Memphis paper that dominated East Arkansas, led with the story of the Dumond castration under a banner headline:

MASKED GUNMEN CASTRATE RAPE SUSPECT
Wife, others say mutilators got wrong man

They ran a photo of Dumond in his hospital bed, holding Dusty's hand.

Reading it in his own morning bed, Hill learned enough about the rape to make him curious. He also learned enough to send him inexorably along the journey that would consume him.

The Dumonds were quoted as saying that the rape victim described her assailant's vehicle as a late-model red pickup with no tailgate. Dumond drove a brown 1963 Chevy with a tailgate. The Dumonds said he was put in a lineup in which nobody else even remotely resembled him. They said the victim identified another man as her attacker, but the charges against him were dropped.

Robert Hughes, reached in California, told *The Commercial Appeal* that Dumond couldn't have been the rapist. Dumond, he said, came home sick on the afternoon of September 11, the day of the rape.

"I was there all day and he was, too," Hughes said. "He got home about 10:30 or 11:00. He was sick. He had been sick the day before—pretty bad.

"I know he wasn't the one who did that. And then they do this to him. And he's messed up for life. It's sick."

The story quoted character witnesses who said Dumond wasn't the type to commit a rape. It quoted the pastor at Good Hope Baptist Church, who said Dumond did a good job as youth director.

Dumond's attorney, Larry Horton, told the newspaper that the investigation of the rape was a joke. He said police never questioned neighbors or other possible witnesses, a lapse that seemed strange since the victim said she was followed home after school from the Diamond Burger. The newspaper also quoted Conlee, who said investigators were "up against a blind wall" on the castration investigation. He had no suspects and felt there wasn't a link between the castration and the victim's family.

Through the news reports and his own observations, Hill noted that the castration happened just after Dusty Dumond's letter defending her husband had been printed in the local newspaper. The castration also coincided with demands for an investigation of Conlee's activities as sheriff, prompted by Hill's reports.

Floyd French, a member of the local quorum court (the administrative board of the county), had called for a special prosecutor to look into possible illegal activities, including drug dealing, involving the sheriff's office. He said a special prosecutor was needed because the local prosecutor was "not on our side." Fletcher Long, deputy prosecutor for Forrest City and Raff's deputy, gave a blistering, swift response. "They can request, I guess, for somebody to fly to the moon. But they don't have the authority." Either Long's boss, Raff, would have to step down and ask for a special prosecutor, or else a circuit judge would have to appoint one. "There is nothing to be pursued," Long concluded.

To Hill, Long's comments were troubling but not surprising. Conlee had already identified Long as his personal attorney. When Hill told Conlee he was going to air reports on the sheriff's office, Conlee told Hill he should call his attorney, "Fletcher Long."

Though Hill was at first reluctant to get involved in the castration and rape case, he would come to realize he had little choice. It may have sounded corny to some, but Hill took his First Amendment responsibilities seriously. He already had a network of sources in St. Francis County. He had information on Conlee. He had to stay involved. He had to fight for justice.

On the Tuesday after the castration, *The Commercial Appeal* had its fourth front-page story on the castration in four days. It was an interview with the rape victim's father, the county cornoner, the owner of a local funeral home, part of the establishment, part of the old money. Hill knew who he was, though no one in the news media was using his name—yet. The father had been at the University of Arkansas when Hill was, but Hill hadn't known him. However, Hill had been very familiar with the woman the father married. She was a majorette for the Razorback marching band, a campus beauty, and an ROTC sponsor.

The father told the press the castration was a "very, very stupid move on someone's part. . . . My rights have been violated. His [Dumond's] rights have been violated. We're both victims." He called the castration "mind-boggling." "I didn't do it," he said. "I didn't want it to happen." Conlee claimed the sheriff's office had looked into more than one hundred leads on the castration, yet turned up nothing.

Over the next weeks, the press began to take a harder look at Dumond. The press said he had been accused of murder in a claw hammer attack in Lawton, Okla. It was his past again. His past always came back. The report was true, Dumond was forced to admit. He told reporters he had known the attack "was fixin' to happen," and said he didn't try to stop it. But he denied swinging any blows. The charge was dropped when he testified against the others involved. In one report on Dumond, an article quoted a psychiatric profile of Dumond that said he had an inferiority complex and needed to "constantly prove to himself his own masculinity."

There was more, some of it perhaps even more troubling than the murder charge. Dumond had a long history with drugs, the papers said. And—in 1976 he had been charged with another rape. A sheriff's deputy said the charges were dropped when the woman refused to testify, though Dumond had pretty much admitted he was guilty.

Hill had to admit to himself that Dumond might be the kind who would rape a Forrest City teenager after all. If a rapist is castrated, who's going to sympathize with the rapist? Was Hill doing the right thing to investigate? Maybe, maybe not. But if the sheriff or his vigilantes were involved, it wasn't the right kind of justice.

In any case, perhaps all his soul-searching was a waste of time. Hill might not have known it, but it was too late for him to turn back now.

Eight

Hey, they was blood everywhere. They was blood all over
the floor. It was so thick; you know how blood gets real
slippery. There was blood all over the cabinets, the floor,
the ceiling. And I got outa there.

—Wayne Dumond

Coolidge Conlee thought Marcy Halbert was a cute sprite.
She worked in the tax collection office at the front of the
sheriff's department in the St. Francis County courthouse.
She was a petite dishwater blonde with a pageboy. Conlee
liked to flirt with her. He called her "Little Bit," and he would
do a lot to impress her. He once offered her a trip to Vegas
to gamble, but she refused.

A few days after the castration, Conlee came out of his
office to her desk. "Little Bit, come back to my office. I got

somethin' I want you to see." She walked in and he shut the door.

From his desk drawer he pulled out a quart jar, with a little bit of formaldehyde running around the bottom. He held it up to her and spun it around. Inside were Dumond's testicles. She looked at him, and back at the jar. "What is it?"

"Them are Dumond's nuts," he said, and grinned that sheepish grin.

She looked again. The liquid was pinkish, the testicles were lighter and misshapen, and they seemed as big as golf balls. Her mouth was open. "Oh, okay." Very good, sheriff.

"Be sure and don't tell anybody about this, because this is a federal offense, and I could get in trouble for showing it to you." (Conlee was wrong. There is no law against showing body parts.) The sheriff smiled at her. She was about to puke.

O'Neal Webb, a crusty, old Forrest City resident who visited the sheriff about his son's troubles with the law, also got a view of the testicles from Conlee. Conlee called Webb into his office during one of Webb's visit to the courthouse. He held up a jar full of liquid.

"What is it?" Webb asked.

"Why, you know what that is; that's the boy's nuts!"

Webb said the sheriff told him this was what happened if you raped the wrong girl in his county. Webb was the one who told Conlee it was against the law to show the body parts. But Conlee just said they were "evidence." Poor Conlee. He left bootprints wherever he walked.

O'Neal Webb was only too happy to talk to Hill about the sheriff showing off the testicles. Marcy Halbert was a little scared, but she talked, too. Marcy said the father of the rape victim had visited the sheriff's office quite a bit before the castration. He and the sheriff were apparently friends. After the castration, he wasn't seen there very much.

Hill also talked to Bill Gatling, the longtime circuit clerk, who saw the sheriff in the courthouse parking lot holding up a jar filled with liquid, clouded with blood. Conlee told Gatling, too, that Dumond's testicles were in the jar.

Needless to say, Conlee's actions caused the rumor mill to work overtime in St. Francis County. It was all over town about the sheriff fooling around with Wayne Dumond's nuts. He had 'em everywhere, people said, at a wedding, in the back room playin' craps with 'em, the whole bit.

Hill could never prove any of that. But Hill had plenty of evidence about Conlee's other fun and games. Perhaps it was the sheriff's arrogance that made it so easy for Hill to find stuff on him. Conlee simply believed he *was* the law, and the law could not be touched.

Trouble was, Coolidge didn't realize he couldn't even trust the people around him. Robert Smith, the constable, started calling Hill with tips. Then Hill started calling Smith. Smith had not seen the testicles but he told Hill that he knew Conlee had gone by the funeral home—the one owned by the victim's father—to get something to put the testicles in. Smith said Conlee called the sheriff's office on the radio and asked a funeral director to meet him there. Smith said Conlee was met by Regan Hill, an employee.

As a reporter Hill had no choice but to call the victim's father with this information, to see if he could get a reaction. Hill was amazed at the response. Yes, said the victim's father, Regan Hill did provide the formaldehyde used to preserve the testicles. Yes, said the father, he had seen the testicles at the funeral home.

The case was getting unreal. What had been an investigation into a possibly corrupt sheriff's office was now a journey into hell. And now, Hill's network of sources was really beginning to pay off. He developed a good relationship with State Police Capt. Fred Odom, an honest local state police officer based in Forrest City. Odom kept Hill informed about the investigation of the castration—which was turning up nothing—and about alleged gambling in the sheriff's office.

But as far as Hill was concerned, it wasn't just alleged. It was real. For in addition to helping Jack out on the testicle display, Marcy Halbert helped Jack develop solid leads on the gambling. The sheriff and his buddies threw dice in the sheriff's office, she told him. One game they played was high dice. The highest roll won, but sevens busted. She said Conlee sometimes played with crooked dice. Once he showed her how he switched them, with a little sleight of hand. In one game, constable Robert Smith lost more than one thousand dollars to Conlee on a single roll.

Halbert had other tales. After the castration, she said, over and over Conlee told anyone who would listen that Dumond castrated himself. To Halbert, it was almost as if he was obsessed with the idea. She told him it was impossible.

"Naw, he got real drunk and on drugs, and he did it," he responded.

She laughed. "If you're that drunk, you're passed out."

There was one other notable event around town at about this time. There was a cheerful wedding, where Sambo Hughes, Conlee's chief deputy, married Dora Flanagin, the sister of local state representative Pat Flanagin. The local paper noted that Conlee and his wife were in attendance.

It might seem a minor event, not even worth mentioning. But it put the Flanagins in the web. The state representative would later be known publicly as an ally of Conlee's. His sister would later swear that the sheriff routinely broke the law.

No matter how hard he tried, Dumond would never outrun his past. After he got back from Vietnam, Wayne met his first wife—Lawanda Jean Strain—on leave, while she was working behind the counter at a DeWitt hamburger joint. The marriage didn't work, but she gave him his sons. He married her, he would say later, on the rebound, after his high-school love ditched him. And he would also say that he reinlisted in the army on the rebound. It was another decision that would cost him.

Now a staff sergeant, Dumond was stationed at Fort Sill, near Lawton, Oklahoma, a dusty, grimy town, not unlike Forrest City, Arkansas. It was 1972. He became friends there with a man named Bill Cherry. They were both in advanced individual training, teaching young men how to shoot cannons. Wayne's Vietnam tour was over. He still liked to drink and do drugs, partly as a result of Nam.

Dumond and Cherry drank and partied together. They even spent a Christmas together. Cherry had come back from Germany, where he was stationed, with a German wife and two adopted German children. They also had two children together.

A fellow by the name of Albert Jackson, another drinker and a brawler, made their acquaintance. He liked German women, and he liked Bill's wife. This turned out to be a fatal weakness, for Cherry and Dumond came up with a scheme to kill Jackson.

Maybe for Dumond, just back from Nam, life didn't seem quite as precious, especially the life of a man messing around with his buddy's wife. Or maybe it was all the drinking and the drugs that made him a little bolder. Or maybe it was just in Dumond's nature to get into trouble.

As Cherry and Dumond were drinking at Wayne's house, one of Cherry's adopted children, a grown woman by now, was to slip drugs into Jackson's coffee, to knock him out. Another man, a Bill Hines, was to join them. As soon as Jackson was knocked out, Cherry told Dumond, they would go over to the house and kill him. Somebody produced a couple of what Dumond would call "breakover bars," steel bars that are effective for beating.

Dumond has a low, flat, Southern Arkansas drawl, with a shifty, understated manner of speaking that lets a listener know he's done time. Here's how he tells this story.

> I don't know where Bill Cherry got the hammer. But Bill Hines walked off into the house, busted the guy in the back of the head with one of these things, these breakover bars. Bam! Busted his head all open. For whatever reason, when Bill Cherry saw that first little dab of blood he just went berserk. He lost all control of hisself, and took that clawhammer and beat that man to death. There was no life left in him. . . . He broke that clawhammer on the back of his head.

Dumond watched every lick.

> Wow. It was like a dream. Imagine two guys walkin' right here and all of a sudden one of them just starts beatin' the other one in the head with a hammer. And just beats

him down on the floor and just keeps beatin' him and
beatin' him and beatin' him. What're you gonna do? I was
thinkin' gosh, you've hit him enough, man.

Hey, they was blood everywhere. They was blood all
over the floors. It was so thick; you know how blood gets
real slippery. There was blood all over the cabinets, the
floor, the ceiling. And I got outa there.

Dumond was charged with homicide, but was allowed to
testify for the state. The charges against Wayne were dropped.

That bloody scene was a prelude to what was to come
for Wayne Dumond. Even he saw the parallels. It happened
to him near the kitchen. Both men were hurt. But the biggest
parallel was all that blood.

Dumond was transferred to Washington. That's when
he really got into drugs.

I'm talking PCP, LSD, mescalines. I loved hallucinogenics.
I guess the Fort Sill incident snapped something inside
of me. Oh, maybe it was just everything piled on top of
everything else. Vietnam was right there at the back door,
all this killing took place, and in the military you are faced
every day, especially in the field artillery, with life-
threatening situations. One of those howitzers could blow
up in your face.

That would make some men pause. For Dumond, it made
him charge ahead.

Nine

A free press can of course be good or bad, but most
certainly, without freedom it will never be anything but
bad.

—Albert Camus

The Dumonds finally went home. Neighbors and friends had
pitched in to clean up the blood. Wayne and Dusty were
being peppered with requests for interviews from the trash
press—the *Globe, The Weekly World News.* Wayne was a
freak show. Their story was tawdry tabloid titillation. Their
privacy was gone. Wayne was not only an accused rapist,
he was a mutilated man. Dusty, meanwhile, was a crusader
for his rights.

In the county the momentum was growing for an
independent investigation of Conlee. For many in St. Francis

County, Conlee's leadership was reprehensible. The St. Francis County Quorum Court, the administrative body of the county, was influenced by court member Floyd French's attempts to fight Conlee. The county was in an uproar as the court met to consider calling for an investigation of the sheriff.

The night of that meeting was the night Wayne came home from the Memphis hospital. Dusty went to the quorum court meeting; she joined many of the county's townsfolk and country folk, all of them curious as to whether Conlee would become the subject of an official investigation.

And when she went there, everyone was talking about the most horrible thing—Conlee had Wayne's testicles in a jar, they said, and he was showing the body parts to the people in his office.

Upon hearing this news, Wayne felt humiliation. Dusty felt fear. "We didn't know what [Conlee] would plan next," she would testify later. "When we found out the sheriff had his testicles in a jar, we felt that maybe the sheriff would put my breast in a jar."

That night, as those in the audience buzzed about Conlee's horrible deeds, the quorum court discussed more mundane matters of his supposed official misconduct—the same types of concerns that Jack Hill had raised in his series of reports on Conlee. The grotesque display of Wayne Dumond's body parts was not on the court's agenda. Still, in an eight-to-three vote, the court voted to investigate Coolidge Conlee.

The vote didn't end the threat to the Dumonds. For a while, Wayne and Dusty took turns staying up all night, guarding the house and children. They sat on the porch with a gun. But it couldn't go on. Because of the sick retributions against the family, even their friends refused to take care

of the Dumonds' children. They realized they couldn't live
at home. Their safety and the safety of their children was
a concern, but most of all they could no longer stand the
memories of the house and of the blood. The children went
with relatives. Wayne and Dusty went back to DeWitt, to
live with Wayne's father.

It seemed almost predictable that their empty house
would be burned down. The Forrest City vigilantes had
struck again.

When the Dumonds moved to different residences, on
March 23, 1985, they lost their family. When the old clapboard house was burned down in the middle of the woods,
they lost their home. They haven't been a family, or had
a home, ever since.

That spring, Conlee, Long, and Raff denounced the St. Francis
County Quorum Court's calls for an investigation of the
sheriff's office. "A piece of toilet paper. . . . It doesn't mean
a thing," was Conlee's description of the board's call for a
special prosecutor. Circuit judges John Anderson and Henry
Wilkinson said there was no basis for an investigation.

Hill realized that the Quorum Court resolution might
not do any good. He forged ahead. When Conlee threatened
to sue him and KAIT, he was ready with an answer to the
reporters who called him for a response. "The public's interest
would be served," Hill told the Associated Press, "if Conlee
would file suit against us because he would then be forced
to answer questions in court that he would not otherwise."
He was so proud of the response that he told the station's
Nashville attorneys.

"You said what?" Jon Ross yelled. "I can't believe you
said that!" The attorneys instructed him to merely say he

was careful in checking Conlee's actions and to leave it at that.

Three days later, more evidence mounted that the fire at Forrest City Aviation wasn't just an accident. Larry Dietz, the owner of a Forrest City electronics firm, was charged with buying four two-way radios—a month after the March 1984 fire—from Kenneth Conlee, the sheriff's son and manager of the crop-dusting business. State Police said that the radios were reported as a $1,700 loss in the fire and that two insurance companies had paid a claim on them. Kenneth Conlee was charged the next day with collecting insurance money fraudulently. The sheriff said he was disappointed in his son, but also said police reopened the investigation for political reasons only. "They've been harassing me ever since I've been in office," he said. Raff, the district prosecutor, called for an investigation. Conlee remarked, "That just goes to show you your own prosecuting attorney isn't doing me any favors."

To Hill, this all smelled to high heaven. Raff's investigation was all a mirage to create the illusion of propriety, he thought. Raff's elected position put him over a sprawling five-county area in the Delta and gave him the power to appoint deputy prosecutors in each of the counties. Known for his flashy jewelry and clothes, as well as his big size (about 230 pounds) he was also recognized to be one of the most powerful politicians not just in the Delta, but in all of Arkansas.

"He should have become a Baptist preacher," Conlee remarked admiringly. During one murder trial in Forrest City, the sheriff claimed, the department got nearly two dozen calls from people who wanted to know when Raff was making his closing argument. "They just wanted to see him perform. They didn't care how the case came out," Conlee said.

But Hill's investigation helped him learn there was a darker side to all that. Raff, he was told, was an egotist of legendary proportions. A Delta sheriff told Hill that Raff expected to be put on a pedestal, and if the sheriff didn't buy him a pair of expensive boots or a pistol every so often, he would not be one of his favorites.

Raff lost few cases. Some said he never lost. But some said he wouldn't try a case unless he was guaranteed of winning. One sheriff was frustrated at the lack of prosecution of some cases. In reply, Raff sneered, "If you bring me something besides a can of Spam, I'll prosecute it."

Raff drove around the district in a van that proclaimed his name and title. Hill was also told that on his office wall was a tribute from a local poet:

> . . . friends, you see me as I am,
> The true Gene Raff and no flim-flam.
> Fame came to me—I didn't want it.
> But if you've got it, why not flaunt it?

At Jonesboro's KAIT-TV, manager Darrell Cunningham posted his letter of resignation. Channel Communications would be bringing in its own man. Suddenly, the picture changed, and the implications were ominous for Hill. Without a strong news organization behind him, he was without his right arm.

Still, he pressed ahead. Horton, the Dumonds' attorney, fed him the Forrest City police department's file on the Dumond rape case. There were two statements from the victim. They contained discrepancies.

She told Sgt. Bill Dooley that the rapist taped her mouth at home. In the second statement, which she typed, she said the taping happened in the woods. In fact, in the second statement, she was even talking to the rapist as they left the house. "I told him I didn't want to go, but he said nothing and kept on walking. I told him again as we walked to the driver's side of the car, I don't want to go."

She also identified the rapist's eyes as "deep blue" or crystal blue. But many of Dumond's friends would say his eyes are hazel, a shade of brown.

Hill also questioned the girl's detailed description of the drive to the rape scene. She was supposedly bent down, her head against the seat, while he drove. But she was able to identify every street and turn. The names of the streets are changed in the following account:

> We then drove down Apple to Pine, and turned left onto Pine. When we reached the highway he turned right and drove down to Pennsylvania and turned right. Then he turned right again on Adams Circle. He drove up as far as Dr. —— [name omitted]'s second driveway and then pulled in and turned around and drove back down to Pennsylvania ext., turned right and drove to the first gravel road on the left. He drove down this road a little way and then turned off to the left behind some trees.

The file said a man with a yellow shirt had been walking near her house when she was abducted. There was no indication that police tried to find him or even that they asked her who he was. She also said the rapist had trouble getting her car out of the wooded area where he raped her. She said he tried to back up but couldn't, and made a circle around a big tree and over some bushes to get back to the road. There was no evidence the police ever examined the area for tire tracks.

Officer Dooley admitted to Hill he noticed the differences in the two statements. But he said that didn't bother him because of her positive identification of Dumond. There was no doubt Dumond was the rapist, Dooley said.

Dumond's trial was set for August. The spring was already getting steamy and turning into summer, while Hill chased down a blind alley. As an investigative reporter, he was obliged to check out a report that a local ne'er-do-well had overheard someone brag in jail about helping castrate Dumond at the behest of Coolidge Conlee. Dumond's attorney, Horton, told Hill that the inmate had written a letter to Quorum Court member French admitting he performed the castration and implicating Conlee in the conspiracy. The inmate, an odd-job type named Charlie Hickman, called State Police Captain Fred Odom from jail. Odom taped the conversation and gave a copy to Hill.

> Odom: All right, do you have some idea who put 'em to do it?
> Hickman: Uh-huh.
> Odom: Can you give me at least, uh, one tidbit on that so I can generate some interest?
> Hickman: He runs places, and he runs things up here.
> Odom: Is, uh, you talking about Coolidge?
> Hickman: Uh-huh.
> Odom: The sheriff?
> Hickman: Uh-huh.

Another local tough, Larry Lewis, was also supposedly in on it, according to the jailhouse songbird. In the letter, he wrote, "Charlie told me himself that he was hired by

Coolidge Conlee to casterate the Drummond guy [sic]."

With a little checking, Hill found another man, Jimmy Hobson, who had shared a cell with Hickman. Odom arranged a meeting at his church in Forrest City. They figured a church would be the last place Conlee would go. With Hill's tape recorder rolling, Hobson said Hickman was afraid of being in jail. He was afraid that he might be taken from his cell and killed, and that his secret would go with him. So he sang. "And on, you know, several occasions he had told me about the casteration—such as, you know, the strange look that a man has on his face when, you know, cut his sac open and drop 'em out on the ground [sic]."

The first songbird who fingered Hickman, Tracy Stultz, would pass a polygraph. But Hobson's test was inconclusive, meaning he might have lied.

But there were other problems with the story. Hickman and Lewis had an alibi: hired as temporary truck drivers, they had logs showing they were in another part of the country when the castration occurred. But Hill would spend hours trying to show the logs could have been altered, and that only one of the two men signed the log tickets during part of the journey. It was hearsay, circumstantial evidence, and it proved nothing. Hill became lost in the story, attempting to crack the castration case. Hickman would later recant, when Hill confronted him with the evidence. He said he made up the claims, that he was just trying to get out of jail. The bottom fell out of his theories.

Charlie Hickman passed a lie detector test indicating that he had not been involved. The brags he had made in jail were lies, he said.

Still, Hill pushed station managers to let him air what he had. He knew he had enough to put Conlee's testicle display on the air. He had enough on the gambling. Although he thought he could also tie Conlee to the castration, it was now clear that he couldn't.

But KAIT balked. Testicle display? asked his managers. Gambling? Unnamed sources? It wasn't enough. Maybe the testicle display evidence looked solid, they indicated, but it wasn't exactly family programming.

Meanwhile, local investigators said Dumond's house had been so thoroughly burned in the fire, they had no evidence how the blaze began. Hill, familiar with the details of another apparent arson, at Forrest City Aviation, was incredulous. But he'd seen it all before.

Horton asked Hill if he wanted a gun to protect his own house. He refused. But he later learned that Odom, too, feared for his own family. A suspicious car had been cruising his house.

Then, when Jack went home one night, Anne revealed for the first time that she had been receiving telephoned threats. "The voice was gruff and country-sounding," she said.

"What did he say?"

" 'We know where you live. We know where you work. We know your comings-and-goings. And if you know what's good for you, you'll get your husband off that thing.' "

She had kept it inside her for months, but the pressure was getting to her. It hurt Jack to know his wife was suffering. He figured it was Conlee's people making the calls, but there was nothing he could do.

The station's attorney, Harwell, told Jack he needed to be careful. He told Hill to never close the driver's-side door before starting his car. That way he could survive a car bombing by being blown free of the wreckage. Hill followed his advice for years.

Ten

The truth comes very hard. It is not easy.

—Bob Woodward

Saturday, June 8, about a month before Wayne Dumond was to go on trial:

Hill was at work. It looked as if all his work was coming to nothing. The station was afraid of what he had, but he believed that what he had was the truth. The thoughts rushed him: the thoughtlessness; the horrible display of severed body parts, by the sheriff of the county; the television station's lawyers didn't care about the press's responsibility to tell the truth; they only cared about covering their behinds; the arrogance of Conlee—to think he could do anything and get away with it. His thoughts churning, Hill tried to keep his cool. He had to get up and walk away. He left the newsroom and went outside.

The sun was setting. The woods near the station were clothed in fresh June greenery. He strolled out to the road, trying to clear his head. After a few minutes, he walked back inside.

Captain Odom was on the line. Hill's pulse raced. Finally, the call had come. "They're at the house!" Odom said. Hill caught his breath. The sheriff and the judge were probably there gambling, Odom said. Deputies were seen patrolling the area, providing cover. Odom said he would provide backup if Hill wanted to crash the party. Hill agreed, but vowed not to set foot on the property. His aim was to stand on the public road outside the house and tape people as they were leaving.

Darkness fell quickly. After scrambling, Hill found a photographer, an Iranian student named Manchehr Nouri-zadeh (Mano), to come with him, and they headed down to Forrest City under the clear Grand Prairie sky, the stars shining over the farmland in the full brilliance of a Delta night. On nights like this one, an elite police force called the "Rangers," controlled by Gene Raff, roamed, enforcing the law as they saw fit. Hill wondered what kind of vigilante lawmen he might find when he got to Forrest City, but he reminded himself that if there were trouble, Odom would be close behind to back him up.

When he finally reached the house on a deserted country road, Hill saw that Odom had been right. Music was playing, lights were on, flashbulbs were popping inside. A pickup was sitting at the entrance of the walled parking lot. Hill and the photographer eased up to the next driveway, turned around, and parked on the right side of the gravel road.

The curtains were drawn, but the photographer shot

some shadows visible through the curtains. Little did he know that this tape would later shock the state.

An old crusted farmer who lived up the road drove by on his way home from a long day and night. When he stopped to ask what was going on, Hill told him that they were just watching the house. "Well, I'll see ya. I don't want to get killed," said the farmer, and he left. The comment was chilling. But they stood by.

After about forty-five minutes, a man came out of the house, got in the pickup, and pulled into the parking lot. It was dark, and he apparently didn't see the news car fifty feet away. Mano turned on the ignition and opened the driver's side door.

Seconds later, a late model car nosed out of the driveway. Mano flipped on his camera light and the darkest night was transformed into brilliant day. No wonder they called them sun-guns. The car stopped and backed up. Then a large, burly man, who Hill later learned was a local by the name of Calvin Adams, walked down to the end of the driveway. Hill and Mano stood there ready to greet him. The tape was rolling, and the dialogue and incident that followed was captured forever. The slight Hill entered the picture, a rather pathetic figure next to the burly, overall-wearing Adams:

HILL: Yes, sir, how are you?

ADAMS: All right. You got a problem?

HILL: No sir. I'm Jack Hill with Channel 8 television. Who are you?

ADAMS: It don't make no difference who you are.

HILL: What is your name?

ADAMS: None of your goddamn business.

HILL: Well, sir, we're here on a public road, observing this house, observing you. You're on television. You're on television right now.

ADAMS: Don't make no difference.

HILL: Could you tell me what's going on inside the house?

ADAMS: Yeah. We're having a birthday party.

HILL: Whose birthday?

ADAMS: Delton Cummings.

HILL: Delton Cummings.

ADAMS: Yeah. You want to, you want to see him?

HILL: You're gonna let us in there?

ADAMS: No.

HILL: Why don't you let us in there?

Suddenly, the tape showed the muscle-bound Adams grabbing Hill's microphone. He lashed at Hill with his other hand, knocking the audio recorder to the gravel road in a terrible crash. He pounded Hill, knocking him to the ground.

Hill bounced back up, but Adams had the loose mike and was using the cord to swing it over his head like a mad gaucho, and there was a terrible hissing, whirring sound on the tape. Hill's head was Adams' target, and Hill darted backward.

Adams let the microphone fly. It streaked toward Hill's head like a torpedo. He ducked; it hit his shoulder and bounced off his neck. The microphone flew off the cable and the station's signature clip broke off.

Then on the tape, Adams' face suddenly loomed shiny and large as he attacked Mano. He lunged for the camera and Mano was helpless, festooned with camera gear and crushed against the car. That was when the tape went black. But the assault continued.

Adams jerked the camera away from the photograher and Mano yelled, "C'mon, Jack, let's go!" Mano slipped behind the wheel of the news car and slammed the door. But Adams had gone berserk. He smashed the camera against the windshield, cracking the glass. The camera exploded; its pieces flew everywhere. Adams smashed it again; the windshield glass screeched and groaned. The camera broke apart.

With Adams hovering, Hill couldn't reach the car. Suddenly, Mano shifted into gear and sped away. The news car's taillights disappeared into the black night.

Hill stood motionless, barely breathing. Adams turned away from him, and at that instant he knew he got a break: Adams apparently thought Hill had escaped in the news car. Slowly, Adams picked up the camera pieces and went back into the house.

Hill, bruised and shaking, wondered where Odom was. As he walked away from the scene, he hid in pine trees from a car that eased past him. Hill wondered if it was Odom, but didn't dare call out. He waited in the weeds, still watching the house. But he was unable to see who was leaving the "birthday party."

He waited for what seemed like hours. A bird began singing and he thought it was close to morning. Then he decided to try to get a closer look at the house again. As he inched toward the driveway, his feet in the gravel sounded like exploding firecrackers. He considered taking off his shoes, but decided against it in case he had to run.

As he approached the house, he saw a pickup in the driveway. Then out of nowhere, a car with flashing blue lights approached him from behind. Thinking it might have been one of Conlee's deputies, he started to run. Hill dove into the weeds at the edge of a field just past the gambling house. A dog began to bark. Then he heard the soft drawl calling, "Jack? Jack?" It was Odom. A trooper pulled in behind him. "Jack! Are you okay? Are we glad to see you! We thought we might find you in a ditch! I was afraid you were dead." The officers were carrying shotguns and assault rifles.

Hill finally made it out of Forrest City the next morning —with a State Police escort. He knew what his lead story would be the next night. But things had changed again for Jack Hill. His photographer fled the state. There would be round-the-clock guards at his house and at the station. And Jack Hill's name would become even more well known in Forrest City and across Arkansas.

Anne Hill had spent the day and night in Little Rock and had heard nothing about what happened. It was 2 A.M. when she walked in the door at the Hills' house in Jonesboro. Immediately the phone rang. It was Bill McDonald, the station manager at Jack's station.

"Anne, you'd better sit down."

She tensed.

"Jack's okay, but he's been beat up. You might as well come over to my house. Several people from the station are over here, and we've been talking to Jack by phone. He's still in Forrest City."

"Did he get it on tape?"

McDonald laughed. "Yeah, it's on tape."

The tape was carried in a recording box separately from

the camera, a fact apparently not known by Calvin Adams.

Hill appeared on set the next night, bruised, introducing a news story about himself. After it aired, news organizations all over Arkansas and in Memphis picked up reports about the assault. It was Hill's turn to return reporters' phone calls. And, in just a matter of hours, he realized he'd reached a turning point in his investigation of the sheriff. It was the night he went from covering the story to becoming the story.

Anne had once begged Jack, and cried to him, to abandon the dangerous investigation. Now she tried simple reason.

"Look what's happened to us," she said one night. "We don't have normal lives. You've got to stop, Jack."

He looked at her helplessly.

"Somebody's got to stop these crooks," he said. "If I do nothing else in my life, at least I will have that."

She sighed.

"What's the worst that could happen?" he said.

"You could get killed, Jack."

The conversation ended. But later that evening, she was chilled after Jack approached her again.

"I've been thinking," he said. "At my funeral, have them play the theme to *Chariots of Fire*."

It was no joke. He felt more in danger than he ever had in his life. But he also felt a sense of obligation to his profession and to the helpless people of St. Francis County. Little did he know that the worst was yet to come.

Eleven

> We spend so much of our time focusing on news events
> of the moment that have no lasting significance and
> ignoring long-lasting events.
>
> —Ted Koppel

Dumond had watched a man being beaten to death. He had
seen death and destruction in Nam. He was gonna live a little.

He was in Washington now, where he was transferred
after the Fort Sill killing. He was high much of the time.
Something about the Seattle-Tacoma area, he said. Drugs
were easy to get and everybody was high. Dumond ran
maneuvers on pot. He fired artillery stoned. At night he
did mescaline and PCP. He mainlined and he drank. Drugs
ran his life.

Dumond said he never had any real bad trips. His mind

was strong enough that he could distinguish what was real. Never mind that his *life* was a bad trip. Never mind that he was headed for disaster. Dumond's war stories involve parkings lots as much as the jungle, weed as much as the bush, drugs as much as gunfire. Here's one in Tacoma, Washington, in the mid-seventies:

> I was stoned, PCP. I went to this department store. I'm comin' out of the store, and here comes this little ol' car—zoom!—zoomin' up in there. I'm thinkin, Wha! I'm trying to get all outa the way. I'm stoned. I'm thinkin', this lady's trying to run over me. Now, in those days everybody carried somethin'—pistols, knives, brass knucks, or something. I was carryin' a knife.

So he took it out and made her look at it.

> "Lady, you need to watch what you're doin'."
> "Eeek! Aaah!"
> She just went hysterical, you know. "Police! He's tryin' to kill me!"
> I just walked over to my car and drove off. Somebody got my license plate. They picked me up later and charged me with second-degree assault.
> I never laid a hand on the woman. I talked crazy to her.
> The papers, they made a big deal outa that.

That was the second blemish on Dumond's record. It wouldn't be the last. His record was part of what made him prime fodder for the sheriff of St. Francis County, a decade later. It made him out to be a common criminal. Was he?

Maybe, maybe not. He thought he was good only at being a soldier, even when he spent most of his time in uniform stoned. He was really just a naive country boy, trying to prove he was a man. If anybody messed with him, he wouldn't stand for it. He thought he could do no wrong.

These early brushes with the law made him believe he was invulnerable. Even after the assault charge, and the homicide charge that was dropped, he got an honorable discharge. He got away not with murder, but with standing by while murder was being committed. He got away with holding a knife to a woman's throat. He got away with tripping on acid and drinking himself into stupors. He got away with it and he was a hero in Nam. He had some good buddies, and he got some decorations.

What would have happened if the law had told Wayne Dumond early on, enough is enough? What if he had done hard time and been forced to pay for his early sins? He might never have ended up stretched out helpless in that Forrest City house, butchered like a hog. But then again, maybe he would have been there anyway. Some people just have bad luck. It wouldn't be the last time that the justice system failed Wayne Dumond.

Dumond built up his bitterness when he was spat upon after returning from Nam. He thought the antiwar protesters were cowards.

My Dad was a Marine, and once a Marine always a Marine. My Dad is all about God and country. The schools that I went to, they taught patriotism. I grew up patriotic. I was a patriot in the military. I believed in that war. I still believe I did the right thing. Uncle Sam called me, and I went, and I did the best that I could do. It hurt a lot of people, not just me, it hurt a lot of people deep down inside that there could be so-called American citizens

out here saying, "Hey government, you're doing something
that's wrong, here. We don't like what you're doing." That
was not the way that I grew up believing. That wasn't
the way to conduct oneself; they simply didn't teach that.
Duty, honor, and country was what the military was all
about. My country called me to go to war. It didn't matter
where that war was being fought. I took my orders from
the general and I carried them out the best way I could.
Yeah, it bothered me a whole lot. Antiwar protesters goin'
off, people burnin' their draft cards, people goin' off to
Canada to avoid the draft, burnin' the flag, and all this.
The World War II and the Korean soldiers came back
heroes. The Vietnam veteran came back a baby-killer.

Back in DeWitt, that hotbed of the Delta, he rented a house
with Lawanda. There was a woman who lived across the
street from them in an apartment complex. He knew her
from high school. Sometimes she'd be out in the yard. She'd
wave, he'd wave.

One day he went over to her house when he was drunk
and stoned. Dumond would claim years later that he couldn't
remember exactly what happened there in DeWitt. "She said
I raped her. I don't believe she resisted."

Some would believe that, some wouldn't. The truth is,
though, that the alleged victim in this case waited at least
two weeks before she called police and reported the rape.
Dumond was picked up and he spent forty days in jail. Then
she dropped the charges. He never received any explanation
of why. He never talked to her again.

Dumond said he remembered having sex with her on
her bed. If she did resist, he said, "It wasn't much. I wouldn't
have hurt her." Is Dumond lying? If he is, why not just

deny it flat out? Instead, he says he can't recall exactly. What kind of defense is that, particularly when he knows he faced another rape charge years later?

Was the rape charge in DeWitt connected to the charge in Forrest City? It certainly didn't help. Once he was identified as the assailant of the high-school girl, and police ran his record, they discovered the old charge. That probably helped convince them they had the right man. They closed their eyes to other possibilities, and Dumond was made a scapegoat.

Hill, like others, wondered why Dumond, a man with a checkered past and questionable morals, should draw any sympathy. Here was a man who was charged in one rape, convicted in another, a man who abused drugs, who killed Vietnamese for sport, who made trouble for his stepmother because it was fun. If he got caught up in a criminal justice system that didn't treat him very fairly, whose fault was it, really?

There would be many answers. Hill didn't know if Dumond was guilty of the first rape. But Hill suspected there would be a fatal flaw in the second rape case, a flaw so serious that it indicted the means of the powerful in St. Francis County. To Hill, it was the second rape, and the retribution against Dumond that followed, that defined the terror in the Delta he was fighting. It was the second rape charge that illustrated an abuse of power seen only on rare occasions in the United States. It was that rape charge that led to one of the most egregious violations of a man's civil rights in U.S. history.

Of course, it was Dumond's spotted life, his sense of invulnerability, and his skewed conception of his manhood that led to those horrible days in Forrest City. For a man's life is not one event, but a chain of events; each of his actions in one instance influences and leads to his actions in another. He may not see any consequences the first time, but eventually, unless he changes course, he will. To Hill this became a story of that inexorable movement of fate. It was what drew Dumond down a path of horror. It was what brought Hill into the Dumonds' life. Slowly, but surely, it was consuming him.

When Jack learned of Dumond's first rape, he doubted the wisdom of sticking up for Dumond. But he forged ahead not for Dumond's sake, but for his own, and for the people of St. Francis County. He decided to take on the system, and he would come out forever changed.

Twelve

The only security of all is a free press.

—Thomas Jefferson

In the humidity and heat of a St. Francis County night, Dan Malone nervously paced outside his nightclub, waiting for the county's chief deputy, Sambo Hughes. Along the Delta roadside, the crickets were making a racket. Inside the beer parlor, black men laughed and joked as they racked up pool balls and threw dice, safe from the clutches of the law. Finally, the deputy pulled up. Malone handed him an envelope full of money. Hughes's wife, Dora Flanagin Hughes, would say she saw such a transaction occur.

It was only one of Hughes' several stops that week, only one of hundreds of stops he made while preying on the fears of the black people of St. Francis County. And each time, after making those stops, he paid Coolidge part of the proceeds.

It had been during one of their long road trips that Coolidge came up with the plan to take money from the club owners. In exchange for paying him, they were allowed to have gambling at the clubs. In the parlance of the federal courts, the scheme was called extortion. In street talk it was a shakedown. And Conlee let his friend, Hughes, do the dirty work. "If they play, they pay," Conlee told him.

Jack Hill, still a little shaken from his beating, was on the phone in the newsroom when the new station manager, Bill McDonald, demanded to see him in his office. The news editor was on one end of the couch, the station's business manager on the other. McDonald told him to shut the door.

"Isn't it true we agreed you'd only go to that house if there was a State Police escort down the road?" Hill stared at him. McDonald knew what had happened. He didn't want an answer. Hill looked at the other men in the small office. "What's all this about? We've already gone over what happened." McDonald pushed a piece of paper across his desk. It was a list of demands.

The two major points were direct: Hill was to be taken off the St. Francis County stories. He was to agree not to take any more phone calls involving St. Francis County. He saw at once that these were intolerable conditions. He had no choice but to resign. McDonald did nothing to dissuade him.

Initially, Hill's reaction was relief, but as he was going home, he was contemplating the seriousness of his situation. Anne also no longer had a job. She had been dismissed from her position at a Jonesboro bank, officially because of reorganization. She had been employee of the year, a rising star. The Hills wondered if her firing had something to do with Jack's pursuit of the St. Francis County corruption.

Hill's resignation, which many considered a firing, caused a stir in the Delta. Publicly, the television station said it would remain committed to the news. But many saw through the charade. A petition was started asking for more responsive management at KAIT. Roy Ockert, editor of the *Batesville Guard*, wrote in an editorial a few days after Hill's resignation, "To cut back its coverage is bad enough. But to back out on the St. Francis County story is a black mark on journalism and a disgrace to the news director who made the decision."

In the *Jonesboro Sun*, one fan placed an ad that said, "Jack Hill is missing from TV Eight by being too good of an investigative reporter. If you want Jack Hill back with 8, please bombard the station with calls and letters. . . ." Hill never learned exactly how many letters the station received, but guessed it was several hundred.

Freddie Christian, one of Jack's Forrest City sources, called Jack and broke down at the news. "You're the only hope we had, and now they got you." It wouldn't be too long before Freddie Christian was crying again.

Jack packed his files and cleaned out his desk. His minister, Rev. Bill Williams, stayed with him the night he was forced out. Hill would reflect later that the minister's gesture was the sort of thing he might do for a bereaved family on the loss of a loved one. He couldn't have known it at the time, but the minister's presence was quite appropriate, for this also was a death, the death of a career—July 23, 1985.

* * *

But the story lived on. Before Jack had left his television station, he contacted ABC's "20/20" about the castration story. When a producer for the show came into the area on another assignment, he met with Hill in Memphis at the old renowned Peabody Hotel, where trained ducks march down a red carpet to the lobby fountain and where William Faulkner had been a well-known drunk. The producer, a mercurial Vietnam War veteran with a quick wit, a shock of white, Phil Donahue-style hair, and an obnoxious laugh, was interested in the story. His name was Charlie Thompson. Hill couldn't know it then, but it would be Thompson's interest that would ultimately help turn around the investigation. Thompson's help would be needed.

Shortly thereafter, the State Police said the probe of the castration had effectively ended because investigators had run out of leads. In an *Arkansas Gazette* story during this period, a "source close to the investigation" said he would "go to my grave" believing Dumond castrated himself. Hill knew who that was, and chuckled at Dusty Dumond's response: "Did he do it before or after he tied himself up?"

Sheriff Conlee announced he was also closing the investigation into the fire at the Dumond's home. Conlee said investigator Larry Hill—the same man who had ruled the fire at Forrest City Aviation wasn't arson—could find no evidence that the fire at the Dumond's home was set deliberately.

Right, thought Hill. But he could take no smug satisfaction in his realization that just about the entire county power structure was lying. He was out of a job, and he was about to be forced out of town.

Thirteen

I begged him for my life for at least ten minutes.

—Forrest City rape victim

August in the Delta is hell on earth. It's hot all the time, either hot and dry or hot and muggy. Even at night, stepping out of an air-conditioned honky-tonk, you feel like you're stepping into a blast furnace. In St. Francis County, the crop and road dust that lifts up from pickup tires and farm fields chokes pedestrians and grimes their sweat. At the railroad tracks downtown, a few minutes' waiting for a train in the summer heat seems like an endless ordeal. The people here become part of the soil, their sweat salting the earth.

In the middle of one of those hot summers, an August

19, court convened in the St. Francis County Courthouse, in the case of *State of Arkansas* v. *Wayne Dumond,* on an aggravated rape and kidnapping charge that would provide high theater for the entertainment-starved residents of St. Francis County. The renovated courthouse was air-conditioned, and the courtroom where Dumond would be tried was clean and well-lighted.

With its spacious offices, the courthouse was a fairly modern, advanced facility for a county seat like Forrest City—advanced, that is, if you didn't consider that just down from the courtroom was the high sheriff's office, where Coolidge and Sambo and his cronies shot high dice; advanced, if you didn't know that Coolidge and Sambo split money from a scheme to get payola from black nightclub owners in exchange for allowing them to operate gambling games in the clubs; and, if you didn't realize that just a few feet from where Dumond was to go on trial for rape, the sheriff had carried Wayne's preserved testicles around in a sandwich-spread jar and shown them off at his desk like a fishing trophy.

The sheriff served as the courtroom bailiff at Dumond's trial. The judge was Harvey Yates, who ruled that the castration could not be mentioned at the trial. Dumond's attorney was the bulky Larry Horton, who called for help from attorney Bill McArthur of Little Rock. (McArthur's wife had been killed in a mysterious flower delivery that had led to McArthur's temporary arrest on murder charges. McArthur, whose story was told in the book *Bouquet for Murder,* was never indicted on the charge and never went to trial.) The chief prosecutor was the flamboyant Gene Raff, but his deputy in the county, the weak-chinned Fletcher Long, would handle most of the day-to-day courtroom chores.

In the 1961 yearbook for the University of Arkansas, the faces of Long, Raff, and the father of the rape victim are together under the listing for the Kappa Sigma fraternity. Nineteen sixty-one was not a good year for the Kappa Sigs. They lost their charter because a test-stealing ring was operating out of the fraternity.

The wan Jack Hill was not in the audience. But the trial was plastered daily all over local newspapers and television, and he followed it closely. During jury selection, Conlee kept a running total of prospective jurors who believed Hill's reports on Conlee for KAIT. Wrote the *Arkansas Democrat:* "[Conlee's] count, which was shown to the media a number of times, showed only two people said they believed the reports."

After the jury was seated, the trial officially began. Some people would later say Forrest City went on trial that day, but they didn't know the county very well. The true trial of Forrest City and St. Francis County wouldn't come until much later.

The castrated Dumond, wearing shackles, was led in. He was solemn and composed throughout the trial.

The opening statements were routine. Prosecutors explained that their case was built primarily on the victim's identification of Dumond, along with serological evidence that, based on semen and blood samples, narrowed down who the rapist could have been. Dumond, jurors were told, fit the profile.

Dumond's attorneys countered that Wayne was a victim of mistaken identity, that he was home sick the day of the rape. What they failed to mention was that they had dropped the ball on countering the state's serological evidence. Had they performed a DNA test on the semen, a key plank in the foundation of the state's case would have collapsed.

Finally it was time for testimony. In the hushed courtroom, Long called the state's first witness: the eighteen-year-old rape victim, a pretty brunette who was only seventeen when the rape occurred.

As Dumond listened with folded hands, she testified that a man with a gun and a paper sack came into her house after she had gotten home from school on September 11, 1984. After tying her hands behind her back, she said, the man made her tell him where her car keys were, then took her away in the vehicle.

She said the kidnapper, after starting the car, got nervous when he spotted a man walking on the street, and he made her lay down on the seat, so that the man on the street couldn't see her. Under questioning from Long, she gave precise directions to the rape scene, even though her head was on the seat. Here is how the testimony proceeded. Long asked her:

How far did he go then?

About half a mile he turned left off that road and went down to the grass. It wasn't very far from some trees and he drove around the trees and some bushes, and then he stopped.

What did he do after he stopped?

He got out of the car and walked to the front of the car and then he opened my side of the car and got me by the arm and told me to get out and we went down a little path there.

Where was the sack?

I think it was on top of the car.

Go on.

He took me down a little path and said, "This will do."

Did you say anything to him or him to you at that point?

No, sir.

What happened next?

He said, "This will do," and he set me down and he was at my feet.

At this point in time were you face to face with him?

Yes, sir.

How far away from him were you?

Not far. I could see him real clear.

I want you to give me feet. Was it like right here or closer, like I am.

About right there.

And you were looking him right in the face?

Yes, sir.

All right, he was standing at your feet and what happened then?

He sat the sack down and he laid me down all the way and he began to take my pants off.

When you say your pants, do you mean your panties or your jeans?

My jeans.

Blue jeans?

Blue jeans.

He took those off?

Yes.

What did he do with them?

He took my jeans and my underwear off and put them underneath me.

After he had done that, then what did he do?

He reached into the sack and got a new butcher knife out.

What did it look like?

When I saw that I started to back up and he said, "Don't worry. I am not going to hurt you."

You were still afraid he was going to hurt you even at that point in time?

Yes.

Then what did he do?

He began to cut my sweater up the middle and he cut both sleeves, and then he cut my bra off.

Did he injure you?

He pricked my arm, but that was all.

All right now, he has removed your jeans and panties and cut your sweater and bra off. What is said or what is done next?

He asked me how old I was, and I told him sixteen.

. . . had there been any tape involved in any of this?

Yes. He was on my right side and he stood up and began to take his pants off, and then he got the tape from the sack and taped my mouth.

What did he do with his clothes?

I guess—I am not—I turned my head when he started to undress. I suppose he laid them to the side.

All right, now he has removed your clothes and his.

Just his jeans.

Just his jeans?

Yes.

What happened next?

He turned me on my side and started feeling all over me and went to the sack and got—he asked me if I had ever heard of a French tickler, and I couldn't answer because of the tape on my mouth.

What did he do with that?

He put it on himself and began to have intercourse with me, and then he stood up and took it off and said, "You are going to have to help me," or something. He kind of mumbled.

What did he do with that?

He put it back in the sack and then he began to take the tape off my mouth.

After he removed the tape from your mouth, what did he say to you then?

He just said, "You are going to have to help me," and then he began to make me have oral sex with him.

Did he say anything to you about biting him?

He said, "If you bite me, I'll kill you."

You are going to have to tell the jury what he did when he had oral sex with you.

He had my head with one hand and just kind of came over me and forced me.

He forced himself in your mouth?

Yes.

Did that last for just a few seconds or could you say how long?

Three or four minutes.

. . . did he ejaculate in your mouth?

Yes, sir.

After that what did he do?

He mumbled something like, what the hell or something, and began to have intercourse with me.

He had intercourse with you again?

Yes.

How long did that last?

About three seconds.

Where was your clothing?

My jeans were still underneath me and my panties and my sweater and bra were either beside me or he put them in the sack. I don't remember.

When he ejaculated in your mouth, did you spit that out or what?

Yes, I spit it out.

When he got through then, what did he do?

He got up and started getting dressed and he was on my right side, and I sat up and I said, "What do you want now?" and he said, "Your life," and I said, "Why?" and he said, "Because you can identify me."

What did you say when he said that?

I started saying he couldn't because I had to go to school and I had homework and I wouldn't let anybody know, and my mother would really be hurt 'cause she was sick and I wouldn't tell on him.

You told him that your mother was sick and you wouldn't tell on him?

Yes. I told him that she had cancer and that she was dying.

Is that true?

Yes, sir.

Did you mention anything about graduating from high school?

I told him that I wanted her to see me graduate.

I presume that you were face to face with him during all of this?

I looked him straight in the eye the whole time I was talking to him.

You were trying to save your life?

Yes, sir.

Later, Long asked her to describe the man who assaulted her.

He was tall, tall to me. He had a full beard, darker than his hair, dishwater blond, and he had crystal blue eyes. He was kind of dirty like he had been working, real thin.

Some weeks after that . . . on approximately October 28, did you see this man and under what circumstances?

I was with a friend and we were driving north there on Washington. We were going to the car wash to wash his car and we were in the left lane fixing to turn left and this truck just goes by and for some reason I glanced over there and I recognized this man driving the truck. I said, "Rob, don't turn." I said, "Go straight," and he turned and looked at me and I saw that's him, and he went on straight and we eased up. We couldn't go straight beside him and we were behind him and I looked at him again at his profile and I was shook up and I said, "That's him," and we got the license plate number.

Did he still have his beard?

No, sir. He didn't have his beard but he still had a mustache and his hair was all combed and he had on clean clothes.

. . . is there any question in your mind about who that man was?

No, sir.

Is the man who took you from your home to those woods and raped you in this courtroom today?

Yes, sir.

Can you tell the jury where he is situated and which one he is?

Right there in the white shirt.

Will the defendant stand, please? Is that who you are talking about . . . ?

Yes, sir.

You realize the severity of the consequences of you saying that that is the man?

Yes, sir.

That is the man?

Yes, sir.

I know this is not easy to do realizing the severity of the consequences. Are you absolutely positive that is the man?

Yes, sir.

Is there any question in your mind about that?

I begged him for my life for at least ten minutes.

The identification was strong, but what the jury would never learn was that she had also identified someone else as her assailant. Horton, Dumond's trial attorney knew that, but didn't use it. Dumond's second attorney would say that Horton was using a "Perry Mason" strategy—he wanted to expose the true rapist in court.

Why? Maybe, said Dumond's second attorney, it was

to make the dramatic rights to Dumond's story worth more. The attorney had agreed to take half the proceeds from those rights for representing Dumond.

What the jury would hear was that another man, a Walter Stevenson, resembled the rapist so strongly that he was put in a lineup. The victim, authorities said, said Stevenson was not her assailant.

After the victim's testimony, the prosecution built a scientific case against Dumond. An expert said no sperm was found in the semen, meaning the rapist had a vasectomy or was sterile. From Dumond's army records came the revelation that he had had a vasectomy in 1974.

The rapist's blood type was A. So was Dumond's. Dumond was a secretor, meaning his blood type showed up in body fluids like semen. The rapist was also a secretor. The prosecution claimed this profile narrowed down the possibility of who the rapist could be to only a handful out of a thousand men. The defense claimed that hundreds of men in the area fit the same categories.

Dusty recalled Horton telling her that the defense did not need to have a DNA test on the semen to determine if the rapist's DNA matched Dumond's. They had a good case without it, he explained. And the Dumonds had invested too much in the case already, Horton told her. She said he told her it wasn't worth the expense. The cost of the test was about $100.

Then, almost out of the blue, the prosecution introduced its stalking theory—that Dumond stalked the victim before he raped her. Though there was no evidence of this, prosecutors brought in witnesses to show simply that Dumond had the opportunity to stalk her and that he was absent from his job on at least one occasion for about four hours.

When Long and Raff argued before Yates, outside the presence of the jury, to introduce this evidence, Horton and McArthur objected. They wanted to keep one of Dumond's former employers from testifying about the unexplained absence.

Here is how that conversation went:

MCARTHUR: I don't want him testifying and I think that is what he is doing here, and I think it is prejudicial. It raises an inference here that hasn't been raised because no one has come in here and testified as to Wayne Dumond having been in this neighborhood or somewhere where this lady was on that date and I don't know that he has. I haven't heard any testimony on it and I think it is prejudicial. I think it is terribly prejudicial to raise an inference that is not in evidence and I move for a mistrial. . . . It has to be established if relevant through some evidence and there is no such evidence of stalking or whatever you want to call it. The relevance as to the argument of counsel is not legal relevance.

RAFF: Did he have opportunity? The state claims he did.

LONG: Your Honor, the key to relevance is that if it didn't hurt, defense would not be up here trying to keep it out.

YATES: Well, gentlemen, the court is of the opinion that it has some relevance and the court will allow it to be introduced, and the record should so reflect. . . .

LONG: And would the court take judicial notice that August 28, 1984 [the day of Wayne's absence from work] was a Tuesday, two weeks prior to the [rape]?

MCARTHUR: I don't know if the court will take judicial knowledge of that or not.

LONG: I am certain the court will take judicial knowledge of that. The court has a calendar.

McArthur lost the battle. The stalking theory became part of the record—and part of the jury's minds.

Fourteen

You know the truth. It has that special ring to it.

—Gene Raff

Dusty Dumond was not in the courtroom to hear the woman accuse her husband of rape: Dusty was a witness, so she was confined to the witness room. However, she had her own unpleasant moments during the trial.

During jury selection, a woman approached Dusty and began talking about canning tomatoes.

Dusty went on downstairs. The next day in the paper it said she had been talking about the case to a prospective juror. The story was picked up by other media. Dusty looked like a jury tamperer. But the woman told the court she had only discussed canning tomatoes with Dusty, and she was seated as a juror.

117

Still, before the trial Dusty had been optimistic about its outcome. "We'd like to take it to trial and show what we've got," she told the newspapers, "if we live that long." Now, with the help of her family, she was getting her wish.

Bobby Dumond, Wayne's brother, testified that Wayne had been sick on September 10, his birthday. Robert Hughes testified that Wayne was still sick on September 11, the day of the rape. So did Jinger and Dusty. Under cross-examination, the skillful Raff made them look like liars.

Here are some of the exchanges between Raff and Bobby Dumond. Raff began by asking Bobby:

I believe you recalled for us a birthday party that you tell us occurred on September 10, 1984. Is that correct, sir?

Yes, sir.

And you tell us he was not feeling well?

Yes, sir.

However, you did say to us that he did not complain to you in any way about that. Is that correct?

That's correct.

Isn't that a rather unusual thing not to complain about illness?

Well, my brother doesn't complain. I have already made that statement.

I know that you made that statement, but answer my question if you will, and if you can answer them I would appreciate you doing so. All right?

Yes, sir.

Thank you. Did he leave early, did you say?

Well, he left about an hour and a half after he got there.

Did you not say to this jury on direct examination, sir, that he left the party early?

Yes, sir.

Had there been any drinking there?

No, sir.

Your brother does drink, does he not?

He has on occasions.

Do you know whether he had anything to drink at the party?

No, sir.

I noticed in the picture there were some cups in there in the picture. Did you notice that?

Yes, sir.

And there was no alcoholic content in there?

No, sir.

But he does drink?

Yes, sir.

Of course, you have no way of knowing if he had any alcohol before he came to the party or not, do you?

No, sir.

You are not in a position to tell us that, are you?

No, sir.

And you are really not in a position to tell us, other than what we conclude, why he left the party early, are you?

No, sir.

And you are not in a position to tell us that after he left the party whether he had anything to drink, are you?

No, sir.

But you are sure about the fact that he did not complain of illness?

He did not complain.

And if you had an occasion to discuss your testimony here that you are giving here today with others—

With others?

Yes, sir.

Just the counselor.

Well, how about your brother?

Well, he—yes, sir.

In other words, you and your brother have discussed the testimony you are giving here today?

Yes, sir.

And you told him what you would come up here and testify to, have you not?

I told him that I would tell the truth, but I know—

But you did tell him what you would come up here and testify to, did you not?

Yes, sir.

Do you love your brother?

Yes, sir, I love my brother.

And if it be within your power would you not help your brother? That's human, isn't it?

Yes, sir, it's human.

And you would help him if you could, would you not?

Yes, sir.

And if it was within your power?

Yes, sir.

Thank you very much.

Then Jinger, Dusty's daughter and Wayne's stepdaughter, testified that on September 11, she and Wayne were sick.

I was still sick and my father was, too. My mother didn't want him to go to work because he was still sick, but he went ahead and went to work. I was sick but I decided to go ahead and go to school, too. He never complained.

She said when she got home from school about a quarter to four, Wayne was lying on the couch, sick. The rape had ended around 3:30 that day.

Raff tore into the fourteen-year-old:

I was particularly struck by the fact that when you were talking about when he was sick you used the words, "He never complained." I was struck by that fact because the witness right before you used those same words, "He never complained." Did someone talk to you about that or did you sort of go over it with your stepfather or your mother, and kind of helped you with what your recollection was of that in respect to your testimony?

I know that of my own knowledge. He just never complained when he was sick.

Have you discussed your testimony with anybody?

No.

Have you talked to your father about that testimony?

No, sir.

Have you talked with your mother about what you were going to testify to up here?

No, sir.

Do you live with your mother?

Yes, sir.

Did you live with your father?

Yes, sir.

Are you telling the jury that you never discussed with them what you were going to tell this jury up here?

We discuss things, of course, but he doesn't complain usually when he is sick.

Your mother had the opportunity or your stepdad had, they had an opportunity to refresh your memory about he never complains as the witness before you said and used those words? Did they sort of refresh your memory along that line?

I know that of my own knowledge.

She wouldn't play his game. Raff was getting exasperated.

I am asking you didn't they sort of kind of help refresh your memory about that statement, "He never complains"?

No, sir.

How long have you known your stepfather?

About two and a half years.

Jinger, is he a drinking man?

No, sir.

He never drinks. Is that what you are telling this jury? He used to drink a little bit around September 11, 1984? Was he a drinking man at that time so to speak?

He was not an alcoholic.

Now I didn't ask you that. I want to know and I want you to tell the jury around that time period, September 11, 1984, the times that you have been testifying about, was he a drinking man?

Not that I know of.

Did you ever see him drink?

I don't know what you mean, drink. Beer or whiskey? I don't understand exactly.

Raff was frustrated, but he pressed on.

Did you ever see him drink any alcoholic beverages or any sort of beer or whiskey?

He might have drank about one beer or something.

So the answer to my question, Jinger, would be yes?

Yes.

I am sure you love your mother, don't you?

Yes, sir.

And you love your stepfather, don't you?

Yes, sir.

If there was some way you could help them I am sure your love is such that it would be normal for you to do so, would it not?

Do what?

To help them if you could?

Yes, sir.

I think that's all. Thank you.

The trial's turning point came when McArthur moved for a delay after the defense's expert serologist was unable to testify because he had been stung by a bee and had an allergic reaction. The expert was supposed to punch holes in the state's serological evidence. Even though no DNA test was run, Dumond's expert was to show that the blood typing from the semen stains and the other serological evidence didn't narrow down the rapist's profile. That, he was to have testified, meant that Dumond or just about any other man could have committed the rape.

In the judge's chamber, Long strenuously objected to a continuance: "These constant delays are making the facts more and more remote in the jury's minds, and to continue this without any proof that there is anything wrong ... would be very prejudicial to the state, and we therefore object."

Judge Yates replied, "Gentlemen, the court is of the opinion that I, all the way through the case, have been lax and liberal in continuing the case and taking adequate time for anybody to reschedule and do whatever they need to do. I don't think based on the facts I have before me ... that I am in a position to stop the trial at this point and wait until tomorrow to conclude it. The motion will be denied."

Dumond was the last defense witness—and its only hope. After taking the oath, he climbed into the witness chair. With those striking eyes that had betrayed him, he stared at his questioners, only occasionally glancing at the jury.

In brief direct testimony, Wayne told McArthur that he was sick and nauseated the day of the rape. After going to work in the morning, he spent the afternoon on the couch. Repeated attempts to reach his employer, Richard Kellum, were unsuccessful, he said, because Kellum's answering machine didn't work.

Dumond testified:

From 12 until 1 I watched a soap opera on TV and I don't even like it. After that I laid down on the bed. I went to my bedroom and laid down and laid there for a while and then went back to my bed. I was just kind of back and forth. I will also say that I made several attempts to contact Richard Kellum and let him know that I would not be back to work that afternoon. He testified that his answering machine was in fact working, and it was either unplugged or malfunctioning that day. It had malfunctioned on other occasions. I wish now I had of went to the shop or something and left him a note or something.

Later, McArthur asked Dumond if he knew the victim.

Only what I have seen of her in the paper. I seen her picture in the paper a time or two.

Was that before or after you were arrested?

After.

On September 11, 1984, did you have any contact with . . . [the victim] at all?

No.

I believe the testimony has been that on October 29, 1984, that she saw you driving, I assume, the truck that we have talked about here on the streets of Forrest City.

I understand that to be true.

Do you happen to remember what you were doing when this occurred?

I had taken my oldest son to the doctor. He was having problems and I took him to the doctor.

She, of course, sat in this courtroom and pointed to you and said you were the man that raped on that afternoon.

Yes, sir.

Is it true?

That I raped her?

Yes.

As God is my witness I didn't rape that girl.

Raff, masterful as always, swaggered to the lectern to cross-examine Dumond, the man accused of raping his fraternity brother's daughter.

His first comment to Dumond was:

Mr. Dumond, you have a very distinctive voice. Has anyone ever told you that before?

Not really.

Are you familiar with guns?

Very.

Is this your gun? . . .

It is my gun. Here are my initials on it.

Did you have that gun in your pickup truck?

I kept it under the seat on occasions.

What did you need that gun for in your pickup truck?

Well, without naming anybody I had been threatened at one point by an individual. . . .

That is what you are telling this jury under oath . . . is the truth as to why you had this gun?

It was for my personal protection.

And on September 11, 1984, did you have that gun in your truck?

I honestly do not know.

You seem to remember quite a bit about September 11, 1984. Why cannot you tell the jury, sir, if that gun was in your truck on that day?

It may very well have been under there. . . .

What is your best recollection?

I don't remember. . . .

Later, Raff asked him:

Where were you living when you came here?

I don't understand that.

Were you living somewhere else when you came to Forrest City?

When I came to Forrest City I was living in Forrest City.

When you came to Forrest City you were living in Forrest City. Where did you live prior to living in Forrest City?

DeWitt. . . .

How long did you live there?

Since I was released from the military in 1976.

You were in the military?

Yes, sir.

And you had experience with guns?

Yes, sir.

You know how to use them?

Yes, sir.

Hold them?

Yes, sir.

How to cock them?

Yes, sir.

And what they will and will not do?

Yes, sir.

You are not afraid of guns in the slightest, are you?

Dumond looked at him intently.

I am terrified of guns.

Is that why you had one with you on September 11, 1984, in your truck because you are terrified of them?

Terrified of what one might do to me had it been pointed at me by someone else. . . .

You are not that terrified, are you? You are not so terrified of guns that you wouldn't keep one in your truck?

No, sir.

On August 28, 1984, do you recall your boss sending you to West Memphis?

Yes, sir. . . .

All right, did he send you there to get a starter?

Yes, sir.

And you were gone some four and one-half hours?

No, sir.

How long were you gone?

Approximately say, 9 to 9:30 until about 12:15.

Did you hear him testify that you were lost for some three hours?

I heard him testify to that.

Is it your testimony under oath and to this jury that you went to West Memphis, Arkansas, and were lost for three hours?

Dumond rolled his eyes.

Sir, it takes a spell to drive to West Memphis, and it takes time to drive back from West Memphis, and I would not say that I was lost for that amount of time.

We are not interested in what I stand here and say, but in what you stand here and say. Let me repeat the question to you, sir. Were you lost in West Memphis for three hours?

No, sir.

How long were you lost?

Thirty minutes.

You were gone four and one-half hours, were you not?

No, sir.

Did you not tell your boss that the reason you were gone that long was because you got lost?

Yes, sir. He gave me improper directions.

And you told him that you were lost for that length of time, didn't you? You were gone four and one-half hours. Isn't that the truth? I suggest to you, sir, that you weren't lost. That you were here in Forrest City at that time. Is that right?

No, sir.

I suggest to you, sir, that you were doing some stalking at that time.

No, sir.

Oh, that's not true either?

No, sir.

Of course Dumond didn't admit to the stalking theory, but Raff had got it on the record. He had planted the suggestion in the jury's mind.

Later, Raff pressed Dumond on why he was unable to work the afternoon of the rape, and why he couldn't contact his boss, Richard Kellum, to tell him he wouldn't be at work that afternoon. Raff asked him:

Why didn't you go to a doctor?

It costs money to go to a doctor.

Are you telling this jury that the reason you didn't call a doctor—you were sick, nauseated, you thought the flu was coming on, and you didn't call a doctor because it cost money to call a doctor?

Yes, sir.

And you want them to believe that under oath. Is that right?

Yes, sir. . . .

Why [didn't you call a doctor]? You were sick. You were nauseated. You couldn't work. You didn't want to get any medication, sir?

My wife is a pretty good doctor. She has often been called the wolf doctor.

Often what?

Been called the wolf doctor.

Wolf was Dusty's maiden name, but this point was lost on Raff.

The wolf doctor?

She is good. She really knows how to take care of a person. . . .

Then Raff moved in to the rape victim's story.

Did you hear little . . . [victim] testify?

Yes, sir.

Did you hear her say that you were the man that came into her house?

Yes, sir, I heard her say that.

Is that not also true?

As God is my witness, as I have already said, I did not rape . . . [her].

Did you hear little . . . [victim] say that you were the man that forced her at gunpoint out of that house?

I heard her say that.

That also is not true?

No, sir.

She said that you were the man that drove her to a lonely area. . . . By your testimony that too is not true?

Yes, sir.

That you were the man who forced her out of that car? Did you hear her say that?

Yes, sir.

That too is not true?

No, sir.

Raff zeroed in. "She said that you were the man that forced despicable and degrading acts upon her."
"I heard her testify," Dumond said defiantly.

Did you hear her testify to that, sir?

Yes, sir.

She is not telling the truth?

She is mistaken.

She is mistaken, but in any event according to your testimony it is just not true? Is that right?

I am saying that she is mistaken.

Did you hear her say that you were the man that made her beg, plead for her life?

Yes, sir, I heard her say all that.

Did you hear her say, that when she said, "What else do you want of me?" she said you said, "I want your life."

I heard that.

And did you hear her say that you had in your possession a gun just like that one. Did you hear her say that?

Yes, sir.

You heard her tell of her mother who was sick and in a serious condition?

Yes, sir.

Did you hear her testimony with respect to the minutes of involvement that took place in pleading for her life concerning the person she was pleading with?

Yes, sir.

From that point in time until the moment that he walked in that house, did you hear her say that she would never forget that man?

I heard her say it and all that you say.

And the best you can tell us is that she is mistaken?

Yes, sir.

Did you hear her tell us about your eyes?

Yes, sir.

Did you hear her describe your eyes? She called them crystal blue?

Yes, sir.

Definitely blue?

Yes, sir.

You did hear her say that?

Yes, sir.

Is that a fair and accurate description of your eyes?

No, sir.

It is not? You don't have blue eyes?

Hazel.

Oh, hazel? . . . Mr. Dumond, in truth and in fact you are the man who kidnapped and raped little . . . [victim], are you not?

Dumond stared him down.

Once again, with God as my witness sitting here right now, I did not rape . . . [her].

You look at me very coldly, Mr. Dumond. You look at me very sternly, Mr. Dumond. You don't turn your head to the left or to the right. Is that the same way and the same manner in which you looked at little . . . [victim] the afternoon of September 11, 1984? Is it, Mr. Dumond?

I do not know . . . [her].

In passionate closing arguments, Raff said Dumond was plainly lying and the girl was telling the truth. "You know the truth," Raff said, pacing in front of the jury box, "it has that special ring to it." Long concluded the state's case with this plea:

Ladies and gentlemen, rape is not a crime of sex. It is a crime of violence. This is a violent man. This is a man who is dangerous to our society. He has inflicted this on another one of us. We hope that the defendant, Wayne Dumond, gets a term of life imprisonment for life for rape and twenty years for kidnapping. He is a member of that part of humanity that has no redeeming value. He is a person from whom mine, yours, everybody else's daughters, sisters, wives in this community deserve protection. Ladies and gentlemen, the state wants you to find Wayne Dumond guilty and give our society that protection.

McArthur understood what was at stake, and what the jury must have felt. He methodically went over his arguments that Dumond simply didn't have the time to rape the girl and get home in time to meet Jinger coming home from school; that Robert Hughes had testified that Dumond was home sick all day; that Wayne's pickup truck was brown and had a tailgate, whereas the victim said the rapist drove a red truck without a tailgate; that another man, who resembled Dumond and had access to a truck that fit the description, also could have easily been accused of the crime. Then he summed up what the case was about, what it meant to St. Francis County:

I look around at the folks that are here, the interest that has been generated by this case, and I perceive that you must feel pressure. The reason I think that is that all shakers and movers are important people in this community; so-called important people in this community are urging you to find Wayne Dumond guilty. Their motives may be totally honorable, but they are nonetheless applying that pressure. It will take a great deal more courage in this case to return a verdict of not guilty than one of guilty. I know that. I am aware of that point. It will take courage for you to say that the state has not proved its case beyond a reasonable doubt, even if that is your totally honest belief. You took an oath in this case. Wayne Dumond, I know, is not politically important. He is not socially important.

Top: Investigative reporter Jack Hill, who exposed the enormous corruption in St. Francis County.

Bottom: Former St. Francis County Sheriff Coolidge Conlee. He kept Wayne Dumond's testicles in a jar in his office. (photo by Lela Garlington, *The Commercial Appeal*)

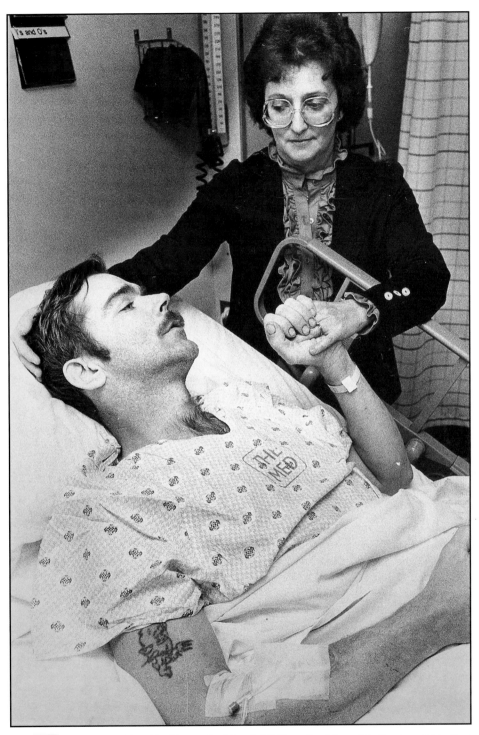

Wayne Dumond and his wife, Dusty, in March 1985, at the Memphis Regional Medical Center, where Dumond was hospitalized after being castrated. (photo by Jeff McAdory, *The Commercial Appeal*)

Arkansas Governor Bill Clinton in 1982, a second cousin of the rape victim. He consistently refused to grant Dumond clemency despite DNA evidence proving that Dumond could not have been the rapist. (photo by Richard Gardner, *The Commercial Appeal*)

Coolidge Conlee is escorted by federal officials from a Little Rock, Ark., courtroom in December 1988 after receiving a twenty-year sentence for racketeering, extortion, and gambling. (photo from *The Commercial Appeal*)

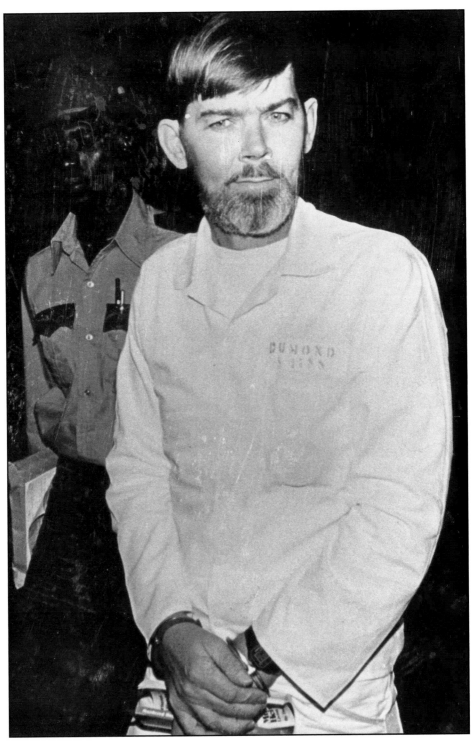

Prisoner Wayne Dumond in January 1989, when he unsuccessfully appealed his conviction for rape. Dumond is still incarcerated. (photo from *The Commercial Appeal*)

He's not financially important. He is just a working man.
That's all he is. He cannot apply any pressure . . . but I
am asking you, and each of you knows that you have
a special kind of courage in this case to return a verdict
of not guilty.

The jury went out for three hours. The Dumonds waited
nervously. Across the Delta in Jonesboro, Hill also waited,
listening to news reports.

It was almost anticlimatic as the jury filed in. Then,
in the courtroom the dreaded word came out: *guilty.* They
polled the jury and each time the jurors answered: *guilty,
guilty, guilty.*

It hurt him, but Wayne wasn't so surprised. But what
did shock him was the sentence. They gave him life plus
twenty years.

Outside, Conlee crowed.

He told the *Arkansas Gazette* that there was interest
in a book and a movie—not about Dumond, but about Conlee.
He said he had been approached by people in Nashville and
Los Angeles. "It depends on two things," he said, "how much
I get out of it and if we have control over it." He thought
it would be a good movie. "Yeah. I'm excited about it. I
would like people to know how I was brought up and that
a fella can change." He said he might play himself, even
though he had no acting experience.

Hill, reading the account, snorted. Wrong again. Conlee's
whole life was an act.

Dumond's appeal bond was set at $300,000. He could
not make it. He was turned over to the custody of the man
who'd waved his testicles around in his office.

Fifteen

I knew you should've never gotten involved with that sheriff.

—Anne Hill

Coolidge Conlee personally saw to it that Dumond was safely transported to Cummins Prison, the grim Arkansas "big-house" made famous two decades earlier by a warden who found skeletons of inmates buried in the prison yard. The story was brought to national attention through the film *Brubaker*, and the secretive brutality and corrupting power portrayed in the movie shocked the nation.

Coolidge didn't say a word to Dumond on the drive down. Upon returning, he remarked to his secretary, Marcie Halbert, that the boys down at Cummins would find Dumond too cute to resist.

To Dumond, Cummins' tan buildings and barbed-wire fences loomed ominous and isolated amid the cotton fields fifty miles south of Little Rock. He never forgot the sound of the doors banging shut behind him the first time. He was to become a troublemaker in prison. He attempted suicide. He spent hours going over his fate in his mind, innocent of rape, outraged, and maimed.

What had led him here? Maybe it was the first rape charge or just the way he had conducted himself. Maybe he deserved to be severed from the rest of society.

He thought of the clawhammer attack in Lawton, Oklahoma. All that blood. His mind's eye saw two big pools of blood—his own and the poor guy's in Lawton. Perhaps this was a strange retribution. He had witnessed a murder, had done nothing to prevent it, had watched blood splatter against the ceilings. His own mutilation was a horrible price to pay, but not so great as a man's life.

Of course, now he was paying with his own life. Dumond was not sentenced to life without chance for parole, unlike the sentence often given murderers. He had a chance for parole, but it was slim. The governor, Bill Clinton, wasn't going to grant it. He was too close to Raff, whom Clinton had made part of the State Police Commission. Moreover, Clinton was part of the victim's family. The victim, he had been told, was a blood relation to the late Roger Clinton, the governor's stepfather. That made Clinton the victim's second cousin once removed. He had a snowball's chance in hell to win parole from Bill Clinton.

His only source of hope was his appeals. His trial hadn't been fair. His expert hadn't testified. Hell, even the *location* of the trial was prejudicial. Just a few doors from the jury box his testicles had been shown before the trial. St. Francis County did him wrong. He had to fight them in court.

As Dumond was contemplating his fate, the Hills were becoming prisoners very much in their own way. They had no money and few prospects. To try to make ends meet, Anne dabbled in bank consulting. It didn't bring in enough money, so the Hills began dipping into their savings. Hill began to wonder why he had taken this course, why he had decided to fight the sheriff.

One day, Jack found Anne sobbing in the living room. "I knew you should've never gotten involved with that sheriff," she cried. Hill buried his face in his hands. What had he done? Where had it gotten him? Conlee was still in office, Dumond in jail. Now Jack was out of a job. The whole experience had been a waste.

Bob Starr, then the managing editor of the *Arkansas Democrat,* was a flamboyant sort, a brash columnist with strong opinions and a straightforward style. A nemesis of Clinton's, Starr had become famous during Little Rock's newspaper war, when the *Arkansas Gazette* fought the *Democrat* for readers and ad money. Starr pulled no punches, blasting the *Gazette* and anyone allied with his rival. That included Clinton, who more often than not was the darling of the *Gazette,* by far the more liberal of the two newspapers.

Partly because of Starr's reputation for brash honesty, Hill approached him with the idea of doing an investigative series on St. Francis County. He waited for months, and nothing happened. Then one day the phone rang.

Starr told Hill the *Democrat* would take him on. For $5,000, he and partner Jan Meins, a former media writer for the *Democrat*, would probe coffee shops and taverns, court records and police documents, in an effort to root out corruption. Their first step was to get hold of the state police file on the castration, since Conlee's file had nothing in it.

The file seemed fairly routine. State police interviews with Conlee, the victim's father, the victim, and Conlee's chief deputy, Sambo Hughes, produced denials that they knew anything about the castration.

But Anne caught a factual error in a statement by the victim's father. He told investigators that he had learned of the castration at a steak dinner during the early evening. Someone had heard about it on the news, he said, and told him about it. The trouble with that story was, the castration was not on the news that early. Hill, a newsman, knew that. But police investigators just accepted the father's account and let it go. No effort was made to find the person who supposedly heard the news report.

Hickman and Lewis, the two odd-jobbers who had bragged about being involved in the castration, were also dismissed as suspects. Their polygraph results were negative. The file quoted Hickman as saying:

> I was just joking and going on with them. I did not castrate Wayne Dumond, and I don't know who did. People have accused me of it . . . and I'd say, "Just for the hell of it." Or, "For $5,000," or something like that.
>
> I told some people in jail the same thing. Tracy Stultz asked me if I did it. I told him I ought to say that I did it, and Sambo hired me.

Lewis's remarks were similar.

I don't have any relationship with the sheriff. He didn't hire me and Charlie to cut anybody's nuts.

Charlie and I were in a beer joint a week or two later and we had just gotten paid for the trip to New York and Charlie was drunk and flashing his money and he made the statement that, "That's what you get for cutting someone's nuts out."

Hill still believed Hickman and Lewis were involved. Logs showing that they were on a truck trip during the castration proved dubious. Hickman had not signed the logs during part of the trip. Hill thought he had shot down the alibi.

He called Hickman with the evidence, and Hickman snarled, "If I see you, I'll fuck you up." That didn't shake Hill. He was now employed by the *Democrat*. He was doing his job.

He called the rape victim's father. In letters, the father wrote Starr and Hill, threatening legal action unless Hill stopped harassing him.

In a meeting with Starr, Hill presented his castration theory, involving payoffs, Hickman and Lewis, as well as the victim's father. Hill droned on. Starr's eyelids dropped. His head sagged. Hill couldn't help but think, You mean I sacrificed my job and cracked the case—for this!

Truth be told, though, Hill hadn't cracked the case. It was abundantly clear he didn't have enough evidence to prove anything. It was, in fact, another stone wall, and Hill was no closer to the truth now than he ever had been.

Sixteen

An irresponsible press has the ability to crush a human being—his reputation, his career, his self-esteem.

—Mike Easley, Coolidge Conlee's attorney

Now blacks is gonna gamble. There's three things—they gonna gamble, make love, and get drunk.

—Coolidge Conlee

Public records are the first and last refuge of an investigative reporter. When rumors lead nowhere, when sources make off-the-cuff comments, the good reporter always probes further into the files of officialdom. Hill decided to check on the records of those accused of drug possession during Conlee's highly publicized crackdown. And what he found was quite simple, but alarming—the accused rarely went to jail

145

or even to trial. One source told Jack of paying off the sheriff to get the charges against him dropped. Another said he sold drugs on behalf of the sheriff.

Conlee, Hill found in the records, stuck a rifle barrel in the face of a state-police informant after finding out he was a snitch. He made him beg for his life, and then he ran him out of the county, charging him with posession. But he told him he could return to the area for $1,000. Three years later, records showed, the man paid the sheriff's office $1,000.

Hill heard that Conlee was seen beside slot machines at a black juke joint owned by Charles Malone, where open gambling was allowed by the sheriff. One night Hill donned a baseball cap—his "disguise"—and went to a tavern to look for gamblers and the sheriff. Although Hill met some rednecks and rabble-rousers on that trip, it turned up no evidence of wrongdoing.

But he scored in other areas. A Forrest City dentist by the name of William St. John told Hill that after guns and a diamond necklace were stolen from his home, Conlee told St. John that the sheriff had paid $225 from his own pocket to get the guns from an informant. To get the guns back, St. John was told, he would have to pay the sheriff $225. He did so, begrudgingly. About a week later, Conlee told St. John he could get back the necklace and another gun—for $600.

But Jack's progress on the investigation for the *Arkansas Democrat* didn't stop Conlee from continuing his assault on Hill's character. The sheriff would not roll over. He would fight back. Jack didn't know it at the time, but the next major development amounted to a devastating blow to his career. On a gray February day in 1986, Conlee sued Hill for $7.5 million, claiming the journalist had libeled him through the series called, "I Run This County."

Conlee's attorney, the youngish Mike Easley of Forrest City, told the Forrest City *Times Herald*: "A responsible press is the backbone of the freedoms that we enjoy in this country. An irresponsible press has the ability to crush a human being—his reputation, his career, his self-esteem." Easley suggested Hill's reports were filled with half-truths, innuendos, and lies. Specifically, the suit said the reports falsely charged that Conlee was receiving drug proceeds, was guilty of arson in the Forrest City Aviation fire, was engaged in bootlegging, and was guilty of election-law violations.

Predictably, the Arkansas press jumped on the story. Libel suits were a rarity in Arkansas, and whenever Conlee was involved in a story, it got good play. Conlee crowed to anyone who would listen that he "got" Hill's job. But a week later, it became truly apparent why he filed the suit: he announced for re-election as sheriff. It was clear that he hoped a lawsuit would discredit Hill, thereby bolstering Conlee's re-election chances. What he didn't count on was the re-emergence of a creditable opponent, a former police officer by the name of Dave Parkman.

Shortly after the libel suit was filed, Hill won a national award from Investigative Reporters and Editors. They cited the reports on Conlee as an outstanding example of investigative reporting.

Through his sources, Jack also learned that Conlee had talked about suing Hill with some of his cohorts. The matter came up at a high-stakes gambling game at a local business, where Conlee gambled. Jack heard that one of Conlee's partners had told him he was a fool for filing the suit, that he would not lie for Coolidge Conlee on the witness stand.

It wasn't much, but Jack took some solace in the fact that he had caused Conlee some trouble with his gambling partners.

On April 6, the first article in Hill and Mein's series appeared in the *Arkansas Democrat*. The series was called "The St. Francis Machine," and in it, Hill and Meins portrayed Conlee as a crook and the county as a cliquish, corrupt power structure bent on protecting him. Later came stories on the inadequate investigation by Conlee of the castration, and a biography of Conlee that recounted his Hot Springs days as a gambler. But the *Democrat* withheld stories about dice games in the sheriff's office. One reason: Hill was told by an editor that gambling wasn't such a big deal; after all, everybody put a few bucks down now and then.

Jan Meins broke what was perhaps the most compelling, most damning story of the series. In a story about prosecutor Gene Raff, Meins told of Raff's creation of "Raff's Rangers," an elite police force under Raff's command. In the story, Clarence Kennedy, a former St. Francis County police chief, described meetings of the Rangers:

> There's a long table, and right at the end of the table is a chair with Gene Raff wrote on it with two crosses on each side. All the men eat down there every day—I mean good meals—and he tells them, "There is no one higher than me than God, and this place is mine, and these crosses represent that I am God here."

The *Democrat* ran a picture of a brown Ranger jacket with its patches and gold badges. Over the left pocket was a badge with the embroidered words, "Prosecuting Attorney, First District, Arkansas, Gene Raff." On the shoulder was an even larger patch in the shape of the state. In the center was a man wearing a white hat astride a white horse. It was surrounded by the words, "Gene Raff—Prosecuting Attorney." Below that appeared the word "Rangers."

There was a mild uproar. The *Democrat* blasted the secretive Rangers in an editorial.

> Its ritualistic makeup, its mysterious initiations, the dinner table communion and Raff's own God-like claims make it a weird fixture for Eastern Arkansas.
>
> For all we know, it might be an elaborate spoof, but it sounds unhealthy to us—especially the "God" part.

Meins also pointed out that before Clinton's appointment of Raff to the State Police Commission, elected officials could not serve on the commission. Raff, as the elected First District prosecutor, would have been disqualified, until Clinton helped push through legislation to get his ally Raff appointed.

Also during the investigation, Jack learned about a judge who covered up his own DWI conviction. He learned about plea bargains for murderers, who were given less time than Dumond. Some of the stories were printed. Some weren't. But the information that Hill did make public was inexorably damaging, to the Delta's reputation and its good-ole-boy system of justice.

With the printing of the *Democrat's* series, the fight was joined. Using his lawsuit as evidence that Hill was a liar, Conlee made Jack Hill the central issue in his campaign for re-election. The Democratic primary—the true election in the race, since there are few admitted Republicans in the Delta— was held at the end of the hot, dry spring.

Conlee went to chicken dinners, to catfish lunches, to Rotary Clubs, and churches—and repeatedly called Jack Hill a liar. He took out newspaper ads accusing Hill of working for Parkman. He spoke under shade trees at picnics, and as men wiped their sweat and women fanned themselves, Conlee said he was a victim of a vendetta by a fool.

Then came the story that was, perhaps, a turning point for Coolidge Conlee. Conlee made a mistake when he granted an interview to Jan Meins; perhaps her blond hair and slight build made Conlee underestimate her or made him want to impress her. She asked him about black voters—the voters he depended upon for election, the voters he had courted through visits to churches, through "tithing," and through (Hill believed) bootlegging and the allowance of gambling. But in that interview, he stuck his sheriff's boot in his mouth.

"Now blacks is gonna gamble," he told Meins. "There's three things—they gonna gamble, make love, and get drunk."

It was a mistake. It awakened the dormant spirit of the descendants of slaves and the slain and the slandered. Oppressed Delta blacks were more educated, less willing to take the abuse of racist "leaders" than they had been during Conlee's early days. They had the power of the ballot. Many had the economic means to make their voices heard. Conlee had exposed his true colors. Now they could take revenge.

When he realized his remark could hurt him, Conlee tried to lie his way out of it. He denied saying it. When the reporter produced the tape, he said the tape was doctored. When an expert said the tape was clean, Conlee said the expert was lying. He said his political enemies were out to get him. The *Democrat* printed a full transcript of the interview, showing him a racist.

*   *   *

Election day was sunny and steaming. It was a perfect day
for the indifferent to stay home and a good day for incum-
bents. Hill was depressed that afternoon, but Anne got some
good news later in the day. Blacks were flocking to the polls.

The vote was close, so close that it was late that night
before the final returns decided the contest. Appropriately,
it was an overwhelmingly black precinct that put Dave
Parkman over the top for good. The black people had won.
They had voted Coolidge Conlee out of office.

It wasn't the end, though. Conlee smiled on election night.
He said he would be back—and he would.

Still, there was more bad news to come for Conlee. Caus-
ing more headaches for the sheriff was Hill's contact with
"20/20" news and the no-nonsense Charlie Thompson. That
summer Thompson toured the Delta with Jack, who had
revealed to Thompson his sources and given him everything
he had. Thompson, boisterous and colorful, liked to tell the
story of one woman's characterization of many Delta residents, living in the backwoods, who she said were called
"Swamp Angels." Inbreeding and poverty led to ingnorance
and illiteracy. Ignorance led to manipulation. It was the perfect breeding ground not just for mosquitoes, but for another
kind of bloodsucker—the power-mad politician who could
rule through fear and lies.

But Thompson wasn't afraid, and unlike Jack, who now
had bouts of depression and self-doubt, he plunged the
investigation ahead. One of his first requests was to get
Jack to introduce him to Conlee.

Outside the courthouse that day, they parked next to

a giant luxury car and strode inside. Conlee was standing by the Criminal Investigation Division room, where the dice games were held. A group of fat cats stood nearby. Hill approached the sheriff.

"This is Charlie Thompson, with '20/20,' " said Hill, and Thompson tried to hand Conlee his business card. Conlee backed away as if Thompson were holding a grenade.

"I just wanted to visit and ask a few questions," said Thompson.

"If you aren't careful I'll arrest you for harassment and '20/20' won't give the truth anyway," Conlee sneered. The fat cats watched in amusement. Hill and Thompson left.

During the same trip, Thompson and Hill met with David Rosegrant, the tough-talking state-police investigator who oversaw investigations in the area. Thompson asked Rosegrant if the state police had made available to Forrest City police a picture of Dumond before he was identified as the rapist. Rosegrant didn't really answer, but turned to Hill and said, "I know my theory of the castration doesn't match yours."

"I don't believe I've ever told you what my theory is," said Hill.

"I believe that Dumond must have castrated himself. He was drunk at the time to deaden the pain."

Hill stood there dumbfounded. Experts had said that was impossible, that only completely deranged people were capable of self-mutilation. Yet here was a major authority, in charge of the investigation, promoting the proposterous theory, the "company line." Hill and Thompson left, realizing they were talking to a wall.

Conlee would not leave power until January of 1987. He was in effect a lame duck for more than six months. But with the sheriff leaving office, Thompson believed it was time to move in for the kill. The sheriff was helpless now against the wheels of justice, or so thought Thompson and the Hills. But they met with more frustrations. One of the nightclub owners who could have testified against Conlee was shot in the head. Forrest City authorities blamed it on the man's wife, but she wasn't charged. Osterman, the state-police investigator who was closing in on the sheriff, died in a plane crash. Investigators said it was an accident.

At the FBI headquarters in Little Rock, Thompson demanded more progress on authorities' investigation of Conlee. In a shouting match with FBI agent Ron Kelly, Kelly told Thompson, "I keep hearing about how corrupt Conlee is, but every time we investigate it, we can't find anything."

Seventeen

A popular government without popular information or the means of acquiring it is but a prologue to a farce or a tragedy, or perhaps both.

—James Madison

One warm July night, Gary Christian, the disillusioned St. Francis County deputy whose father, Freddie Christian, had been one of Jack Hill's most emotional supporters, walked out near a lake and pulled out his police revolver. When he put it to his temple and fired, he fell face forward.

Jack Hill knew, when he heard of Gary Christian's death, why Freddie Christian had cried, so long ago, when Freddie had learned that Hill had lost his job. Freddie Christian had known all along what was at stake. Now Jack fully understood. People's lives were at stake. He had wondered before

155

if this reign of terror in the Delta had resulted in lost lives. Now he knew.

Jack went to Gary Christian's funeral; the casket began its journey at the funeral home of the rape victim's father. The father was civil to him. He thought: There's something about a death that makes people put aside their differences, if only for a moment.

The papers that federal investigators gathered in the marble federal building in Little Rock included the key to the investigation: Gary Christian's diary. In it the former deputy detailed sordid tales of gambling, extortion, arson, drug dealing, and fraud—all of it by Conlee and his cronies. It became the bible of the federal probe, an investigation prodded and surrogately led by Jack and Anne Hill and Charlie Thompson.

Christian, who was sentenced to prison on a marijuana charge, tried to use the diary to avoid jail. He wrote that he had participated in dice games. He also wrote that Conlee switched dice when the stakes got high.

> Coolidge Conlee beat Robert Smith out of $300 with crooked dice at the S.O. They were rolling high dice, and Coolidge was switching dice on Robert. They would only throw 8, 9, 10, 11, 12. There has been gambling on numerous occasions at the S.O. in '82. People that know are Sam, Larry . . . Reagan [sic] Hill, Stacey [sic] Dye . . . Robert Smith and myself.

Sam was Sambo Hughes, Conlee's chief deputy. Larry was Larry Henley, a former chief deputy under Conlee. Regan Hill was a funeral home employee. Stacy Dye was one of the key men who had helped apprehend Wayne Dumond.

Pine Bluff. The very name evokes cliffs covered with evergreens, perhaps a spring breeze, or a walk in a meadow. Don't believe it. Pine Bluff, Arkansas, spent much of its time during the 1980s trying to live down popular listings naming it as one of the worst cities to live in in the United States. Its downtown is ugly and blighted and divided by railroad tracks. Its main attraction is that it's only forty-five minutes south of Little Rock, maybe forty minutes from the Little Rock airport. Pine Bluff's town center is graced by a prominent bust, which is rather startling in its unabashedly busty portrayal, of hometown girl Martha Mitchell, wife of Nixon crony John Mitchell; she was the most famous person ever to escape these parts. The city is flat, there is a paper mill that doesn't smell too good, and the reservoir looks just as man-made and grimy as it is.

Worse is the prison at Varner, near Pine Bluff: Arkansas's notorious Cummins Unit. Slabs of concrete rise up from the middle of the flat Arkansas horizon, making escape nearly impossible. The inmates grow crops with hard labor; they work them raw on those dusty grounds. Governor Bill Clinton himself toured the area in the late 1980s, wearing cowboy boots, to get a closer look at the inmate labor programs, and pronounced it sound. The prison system was the province of longtime State Senator Knox Nelson, who hailed from—where else—Pine Bluff.

For an inmate in one of the county jails across Arkansas, the worst thing he could hear was, "You're going to Pine Bluff." That was where the state prison's diagnostic unit was, often the stopping point on the way to Cummins—

and hard labor. Often, prisoners were held for months in county jails awaiting bed space in the state prison system. Most didn't want to go to Cummins. Rumor had it that men were abused there, not just by guards but by other prisoners. And inmates had died there, without anyone knowing—in the hillside graveyard the bones were there to prove it.

Unlike TV images of prisons, at Cummins most of the prisoners are not confined to small cells. When they aren't working, eating, or exercising, most stay in large barracks, dozens of men bunking in the same huge caged room.

Wayne Dumond got an eyefull early when he arrived at Cummins, his new home. He wasn't surprised by it. He saw plenty of interaction at night, men going at it under the covers or under the beds in the barracks.

Half a state away, to the north, Jack and Anne Hill, unemployed, were slowly sinking into desperation. They couldn't make the mortgage payments on their large house with its many windows and sprawling, tree-lined back yard. The Hills were running out of time, and quietly, at 1708 Merrill Cove in Jonesboro, Arkansas, they were losing their grip on the good life. They had cashed the IRAs, the life insurance, and now their savings were gone. They had no hope of finding jobs; they were more concerned about where their food would be coming from.

When they sold the house, the closing was delayed a week. They had to get a $500 advance from a credit card just to survive. The money from the house would be all they had left.

One afternoon it was all over. The moving van rolled up right on time. Anne started to cry. They headed to Little Rock, the state capital, to try to make a new life.

*   *   *

Lee County is the poorest in Arkansas and one of the ten poorest counties in the country. At the end of the nineteenth century, the economy of plantations and sharecropping gave way to no economy at all. The dirt was all anyone knew.

Lee County was part of Raff's First District in the Delta; if the Delta was low, Lee County was lower. The poor were illiterate, the girls were pregnant. The rate of babies dying before they reached one year of age was higher in Lee County than in many parts of the Third World.

In the county seat, Marianna, Bill Lewellen, a black attorney, made the mistake of taking on the white power structure by running for the Arkansas Senate against a large Vanderbilt graduate with a crew cut by the name of Paul Benham. Benham, a longtime senator who was known to make a racial joke or two, looked more like an eastern longshoreman than an Arkansas yahoo. But he defeated Lewellen easily in the Democratic primary; and because the Civil War stamped out Abraham Lincoln sympathizers and all known Republicans in these parts, if you win the Democratic primary in East Arkansas, you win the election.

One day Raff filed a felony charge of witness bribery against Lewellen, one of the few black attorneys in the Delta. But Lewellen was no fool. He used Raff's aggression to strike back and filed a suit against the entire justice system in East Arkansas, charging its corrupt officials were out to ruin him professionally because he had dared to take on Paul Benham.

Lewellen found an honest federal judge by the name of George Howard to hear the case in Little Rock. He asked Judge Howard to block prosecution against him because, he charged, the entire system was racist and corrupt. Olly Neal, another black lawyer in Marianna, took the stand to testify on behalf of Lewellen. He stated that Raff, his deputy in Lee county, Circuit Judges Henry Wilkinson of Forrest City and Harvey Yates of Helena (Dumond's trial judge) treated black attorneys differently from their white counterparts.

"It's clear to me that Judge Yates is controlled by Mr. Raff and that Judge Wilkinson is most responsive," Neal said.

Howard asked if there were an independent judiciary in Lee County. "No, sir," Neal said.

Lewellen testified that he was told by the Lee County sheriff that Raff would "fix" him.

" 'Gene will see about you,' " Lewellen said the sheriff told him. " 'He will fix [the witness bribery charge] so that you can turn your [law] license in and sell insurance for a couple of years and then get it back. . . . You'll be a good insurance salesman.' "

In a remarkable opinion, Judge Howard ruled that an odious racial cloud had permeated the judicial system of East Arkansas. In an extraordinary move, he ordered Raff to stop his prosecution of Lewellen. It was a major defeat for Raff.

But there was another, more subtle effect of the Lewellen trial. It was perhaps an even worse development for the East Arkansas power structure: Anne Hill had closely watched the Lewellen case, since she had little else to do once the Hills moved to Little Rock. Through the testimony of Olly Neal and others, she became acutely aware of the almost laughable shenanigans of the East Arkansas justice system and of the grave injustices forced on the people of the Delta.

The trial helped transform her. Her conscience was stricken. Like Jack, she thought of her prominent family and what they might expect of her. Was she supposed to just stand by while people were trampled down? Gary Christian's suicide, she saw, was a senseless death. The evil was too great to ignore. So instead of fighting Jack, she would join him. She began to study the Dumond case, And she began exploring other areas of East Arkansas "justice."

One day she confronted Jack in the kitchen. "I want you to see this to the end," she said.

Jack was astonished. "Why?"

"I'm tired of all the misery. If we do nothing else, at least we will have done this."

To help out, Anne started looking into a way to prove Dumond's innocence of the rape charge. Together with Thompson of "20/20," they became a powerful force. Conlee and East Arkansas would never be the same.

Lewellen was also a source for Jack Hill, though they met only once. During that meeting in Lewellen's law office, Lewellen told Hill that Governor Clinton had received pleas from black community leaders not to appoint Raff to the State Police Commission. The leaders understood Clinton to promise that he would not make the appointment.

But in 1980, Clinton lost to Republican Frank White in one of the all-time political upsets in Arkansas history. Clinton, of course, could not live with defeat. He vowed to come back. He made apologies and he made some promises, and one of those, Lewellen said, was a commitment to Raff to appoint him to the State Police Commission in exchange for Raff's East Arkansas vote machine.

In 1982, Clinton beat White—with the help of big-bloc voting in East Arkansas—and was back in the governor's mansion. He appointed Raff, the head of Raff's Rangers, to the commission.

It came down to politics, Lewellen said. It was sad, because Clinton had had nearly unqualified support among blacks. But Clinton always has known what it takes to win.

Eighteen

I called it the peculiar drawer because it was a peculiar
way to accept money.

> —St. Francis County Sheriff's Office
> worker Carolyn Rowlett

Dumond, with that deliberate honey-slow speech, full of
bluster:

Master Coolidge brought me down to Pine Bluff. They
never spoke to me, him and Sambo, Sambo Hughes. They
took me to Crittenden County during the trial. They
brought me back to Forrest City after the trial. I said to
Sambo, "Let me make a phone call." Sambo says, "Lemme
ask the sheriff." The sheriff says, "Hell no, he ain't calling
no goddamn body. He's goin' to Pine Bluff."

I just sat back there real quiet. I figured he wouldn't

163

do anything to me as long as I didn't do anything. They took me to Pine Bluff and the first thing they asked me was, "You got any ememies?" And I said, "Yeah, I got one enemy. . . . He's right there."

Dumond spent fifteen days in the diagnostic unit, then was transferred to Cummins, on September 15, a Friday.

Things went well for about two months. They was workin' the dogshit outa me out there on the garden squad out in the field. And I'm keepin' my mouth shut, tryin' to do what they tell me, 'cause I wanted to get me a job—I wanted outa this place. I wanted out of the penetentiary. That was the foremost thing on my mind. Larry Horton kept promisin' appeal bond, appeal bond. He's goin' to the Supreme Court askin' for a reduction in the appeal bond. You know they set it at $300,000. I couldn't make that, that was a little too rich.

But after about three months, they hung me with a phony disciplinary down here. They said they found some weed, marijuana in the trash box, between my bed and the next bed. But it wasn't my marijuana. But that didn't matter. They busted me all the way to Class 4, and took what little dab of good time I had.

I got hooked up with a guy that could buy. Paid somebody a couple bucks, you don't have to go to work today. So we were foolin' around with that, and we missed a payment, and wind up with a couple more disciplinaries. And wound up in the hole for sixty days. But again, I didn't care. The heck with this.

It was a two-man cell, a tiny and oppressive old dungeon. Along with others in the hole, he got two hours a week on the grounds, by order of the federal courts. It was just too cruel, the courts said, to keep a man in a cage all the time. A man had to walk.

I was in and out of the hole for—I spent two thirties, a thirty, another thirty, and then two more thirties. I've had nine disciplinaries since I've been in this penetentiary and I remained convicted of seven of them. Two of them I beat. At one point I was in the hole . . . I wrote one of the wardens a letter, Warden Reed, and he called me up there to see him.

I was big news then. Big enough. And I tell him, "I ain't done a goddamn thing, and you all got me back here in this fuckin' hole." I was talkin' real crazy. A major was standin' right behind me and I figured he'd whoop my ass anytime.

I thought, Fuck this penetentiary. I'd rather be dead than be in here. If I wanna hurt myself, there ain't a damn thing you can do to stop me.

They asked me, "You ain't gonna run off, would you?"

Run off? Where am I gonna go? You done took everything I ever had. Lost my home, lost my car, lost my wife, my family, my health. I can't even get a decent shot of ass down here.'

Dumond, I'm real sorry that you feel that way. He talked real nice to me. He handled me just the way he had to, because I was hot, I was real upset. He says, "We didn't have nothin' to do with puttin' you down here. Nobody here in this institution is guilty of puttin' you here. But we're gonna keep you here. And you're gonna do what you're supposed to do."

They locked me back up. Three days later they came and put me in mental health—observation. "Check this guy out. Find out where his head's at." So they kept me down there for a couple weeks, and I said, "Man, you better get me outa here. I'm not crazy. I don't wanna be around these nuts. Let me outa here. I wanna go back to work. Give me a class and do something."

"We can't do that."

I said, "You can if I get me a disciplinary."

"Well, yeah." So I got me a disciplinary.

When he got out of the hole that time, he calmed down a little bit. He went back into population, back to work. He met some of the older cons, who taught him the way of prison, the way of survival. He made a friend by the name of Joe Fountain. "He's been like a friend to me. Good people."

Dumond claims he was set up again, and was sent back to the hole. After thirty days, he was out again.

A boy in mental health told me, "If you inject saliva into a muscle, it'll become infected and you'll have gangrene." One of these crazy inmates in mental health told me, "Now, if you take that same saliva, and you inject it into a vein, it'll kill you." Makes sense. Gangrene set up in your bloodstream, kill ya. And I'm suicidal as hell, about that time.

Now, I came down here in a state a shock. That shock wore off, and it turned to anger. I vented that anger on the warden, the major, field riders, anybody. Never an inmate; inmates didn't do this to me. And I had a real, real bad reputation for a long time.

I got hold of a syringe and I filled that syringe up with pure saliva. Shoosh! Mainlined it. I just kicked back in my bed and went to sleep. And I was madder than hell when I woke back up the next morning! Made me a little nauseous. But I was supposed to be dead!

Such was Dumond's fate. Couldn't even commit suicide right.

As if to add to his misery, his great romance with Dusty was suspended, for the time being. She divorced him because the insurance rates were too great for a wife of a convict. But she said she still loved him. They kept writing. Dumond became an accomplished letter-writer.

Aware of Hill's association with the *Democrat,* Dumond tried a letter to the newspaper:

> During the trial I . . . established my whereabouts on the day someone was to have raped this girl. The prosecuting attorney called them liars because of minor contradictions in their testimony. . . .
>
> The accuser had major contradictions in her statements, then contradicted them with her testimony on the stand. Why wasn't she accused of lying, which she successfully did?
>
> . . . why me? Why did I have to be castrated? Why my home burned, my job taken from me? . . . No man is safe if that's the way justice works.

Before the Arkansas Supreme Court, Larry Horton, Dumond's attorney, argued that Dumond's conviction should have been reversed. One argument concerned a fingerprint report not disclosed by the prosecution before the trial, which showed Dumond's fingerprints were *not* found in the girl's car, which had supposedly been used by Dumond to transport the girl to the rape scene. Under the rules of evidence, prosecutors are obliged to disclose all evidence to the defense, but in this case the report was not disclosed. Horton said that failure was grounds for a mistrial.

Another of Horton's arguments was that a state serologist was allowed to testify on matters outside his expertise and that a continuance should have been granted to allow the defense to present its own serologist. Horton also argued that some of the prosecution evidence—including the so-called "stalking" theory—was irrelevant.

Before the close of the year, in a six-to-one vote, the Supreme Court rejected all the arguments and upheld the conviction.

John Wesley Hall, Jr., a Little Rock attorney with an unruly mane of curly hair and a penchant for iconoclasm, had developed a reputation as one of the best criminal defense attorneys in the state. To Charlie Thompson of "20/20" it was logical that Hall take on Dumond's case. The notoriety of Conlee, the outrage of the castration, the corruption of East Arkansas—all these elements made the case a perfect one for a crusader like Hall.

Everyone who knew Thompson said he had a way of persuasion. If he couldn't cajole or coddle, he would strong-arm. But it didn't take much to convince Hall. Although the Dumonds had no money to pay a high-priced lawyer like Hall, he agreed to take the case. As a bonus, Hall also gave Anne an outlet for her new-found enthusiasm on the investigation: she was able to work for him part-time, focusing on the Dumond case.

That January, Dave Parkman was sworn in as the new sheriff of St. Francis County. He said his goal was to restore trust to the sheriff's office. Conlee put on a good front. "I've enjoyed being sheriff," he told *The Commercial Appeal*, the Memphis newspaper. "I came in smiling and I'm going out smiling."

Six weeks later, *The Commercial Appeal* abandoned its

kid-gloves treatment of the sheriff. Staff reporters Lela Garlington and William C. Bayne, in a front-page story, wrote the following account:

SOME SAY CONLEE WAS IN ON GAME
Office gambling detailed

FORREST CITY, Ark.—Two plastic dice clicked against a concrete block wall, then tumbled to a slick tile floor.

It was a dice game that began in fun, to decide who would pay for lunch, but the game grew to sizable sums, participants say.

It happened in a room directly across the hall from the sheriff's office in the St. Francis County Courthouse while Coolidge Conlee was sheriff, say office workers and visitors who participated.

The game, a daily ritual for more than three years, involved law enforcement officers, office workers and businessmen from Forrest City, participants say.

It was a damning report. *The Commercial Appeal* identified Danny Burns, the roustabout who Hill had thought might have been involved in the Forrest City Aviation fire, as a player. It also mentioned Dora Flanagin, sister of the state representative and wife of Sambo Hughes, as another person connected with the game, if only for lunch. In addition, Deputy Prosecutor Long was described as an observer and player, for lunch, but Long denied it. He said he'd never had lunch over there, adding, "I'm not involved in that."

The newspaper had other stories about a so-called "peculiar drawer" in the sheriff's office, from which Chief Deputy Sambo Hughes and others would withdraw cash without accounting for it. The money in the drawer came from payments by those accused of crimes, even though no fines had been ordered by a judge. Office worker Carolyn Rowlett told the newspaper that she had learned the cases had been dismissed. The first of the payments—always in cash—was a $1,000 payout in hundred-dollar bills in 1983, she said. She had no way of accounting for it, so she went to Wal-Mart and bought a receipt book. "I called it the peculiar drawer because it was a peculiar way to accept money," she said.

Finally, the newspaper broke another key story. For the first time, Gary Christian's diary was the subject of a news article. His chronicling of the wrongdoings in the St. Francis County sheriff's office became public knowledge.

Hill was overjoyed, but not surprised. He was a source for *The Commercial Appeal* as it broke open the Conlee investigation.

Early in 1987, Dusty and her children stopped by Jack Hill's home. The boys seemed normal—they played with Jack's dog, Bunker—but Hill had to wonder. He thought of Michael at the castration scene, just staring at his hands, surrounded by blood. Could he live normally? How had the trauma affected him and Joey? It worried Jack, as if he didn't have enough to worry about.

By April 1987, even as George Proctor announced he was leaving as U.S. attorney for the eastern district of Arkansas, declaring there wasn't much public corruption in the state, it was clear that some sort of federal probe *was* going on. A federal grand jury was hearing testimony from some of the characters in St. Francis County. Anne and Charlie knew it because they recognized many of the players who came out of the elevators and marched toward the grand-jury room.

Proctor's leaving paved the way for the investigation to really pick up steam. Proctor's replacement was Chuck Banks, a smooth-talking country boy who hailed from the Delta himself. He could not ignore the reports of wrongdoing. He said that he would not stand by while the Delta—his Delta—was maligned. If the reports weren't true, he said, it was time to put a stop to them, and it was time to clean up the region.

In the mid- to late 1980s, Little Rock became the center of progress for Arkansas. Bill Clinton and his hush-puppied yuppies pushed for changes in education, in business, and in government. Clinton wasn't afraid to strong-arm as he pushed for change. He believed Arkansas—still at the bottom of the fifty states—had to take action to make progress. In one fight, the governor embittered teachers by demanding they take a basic skills test—with questions most sixth-graders could answer—in order to sell the common man on his call for a sales-tax increase for schools. In the state Capitol, a scaled-down version of the nation's Capitol, Clinton roamed the halls and pressured legislators to jump on board his agenda.

Still, despite his sometimes heavy-handedness, and his opposite tendency to try to please everyone, Clinton and his allies made Little Rock the envy of Arkansas. The capital city was far removed from the Delta's poverty and illiteracy, from the Western Arkansas rodeos, and from the illegal aliens working the tomato fields of South Arkansas. Little Rock was Bill Clinton's Arkansas. It was the center of Arkansas' commerce, its art, its education, its politics. It was home to the white and wealthy of Pleasant Valley; to the fashionable Park Plaza mall, with its skylights and Christmas lights; it was the operating headquarters for the lawyers and lobbyists who fed off the legislature; and yes, it was the site of Slick Willie's bar in the old train station, where the yuppies shot pool and drank pitchers of beer.

Little Rock slowly became the adopted home of the Hills. It had not been what they wanted. They had preferred their life in Jonesboro, their quiet street, their secure jobs. But now fate had pushed them here. It would push them to spend hours inside and outside the ornate marbled federal building that housed the grand jury. It would push them to keep fighting for Dumond. And, though he didn't know it then, it would push Jack across the path of Bill Clinton.

It was in Little Rock that they finally got some very good news. Three East Arkansas men were indicted in an arson-for-profit scheme in St. Francis County, including Albert Lewis, a longtime associate of Conlee. Another St. Francis County resident, Albert White, with the same monicker as a civil-rights hero, was also convicted of burning his own house for insurance money. It was clear for the first time that the feds were serious about cleaning up the Delta.

After the charges were filed, Lewis told the newspapers the real target of the whole investigation was Conlee. He said the feds wanted him to roll over, to turn in the sheriff. But he maintained, "I don't know nothing on Conlee. I think he's a fine fellow."

To Jack it seemed obvious that the fight had shifted battlefields. He had left Jonesboro behind. Now he was in the big leagues of Arkansas. As if to solidify that point, in July, Hill received news that in Forrest City, Fletcher Long had dropped charges against Calvin Adams, the man whose assault on Hill had been captured on news tape. Long said the charges were dropped because Adams had suffered a stroke. Of course, it had taken him a year to file the charges in the first place. Jack was angry, but there seemed nothing he could do about it. The assault case was over.

Nineteen

Ultimately all journalism is patriotism. If reporters can be said to share a religion, it is devotion to making democracy work.

—William A. Henry III, *Time*

They finally locked Dumond up in what is called Administrative Segregation. It was a two-man cell, like the hole, only he worked and left the cell on a schedule just like other prisoners.

Two weeks later he talked to Warden Reed. "Dumond, I hear you're in Administrative Segregation. What about stayin' in 16 Barracks for a while?"

Dumond just wanted to play with him. He looked at him kind of crazy and said he liked it where he was. "They ain't none of them loud-mouthed dick-suckers down there.

Ain't no mosquitoes. 'Sides that, it's kinda cool."

Reed laughed at him. They left him in Administrative Segregation. For nine months.

Clinton had good relationships with the Arkansas press. His gregarious, friendly style, his ability to communicate in small groups, his beer-and-buffet get-togethers with the press at the Governor's Mansion all contributed to the friendly atmosphere. Clinton, bluntly stated, was charismatic. He could make a questioner feel important, and his grasp of the issues was unchallenged. For any question, the governor had an answer. Some reporters admired him because he could be disarmingly honest off the record, though in his on-the-record comments he nearly always said the right thing.

For the most part, Clinton had avoided getting involved in the quicksand of the St. Francis County-Wayne Dumond story. It had not even been publicly revealed that Clinton was related to the rape victim. The relationship had not seemed relevant in any reports about the Dumond case.

But Jack Hill was getting tired of the piecemeal approach of the federal investigation. Albert Lewis was a small fish. Conlee was the one who should have been indicted. And Jack was appalled at the lack of interest among state investigators in solving the castration case.

One day a routine Clinton press conference was interrupted by an out-of-place question about the corruption in St. Francis County. Why hadn't the governor intervened? a reporter asked.

Upon reading the newspaper the next day, Hill could scarcely believe the reply. Clinton said no one had brought the matter to his attention. "All right, governor," Hill thought. "I'll bring it to your attention."

Hill sat in front of his trusty Smith-Corona and composed a blistering letter to Clinton. He summarized the corruption, listing those who helped cover it up, and also decried the poor investigation of the castration. He told Clinton that some had concluded that he was tied to Conlee and assumed the corruption went all the way to Little Rock. Noting that Clinton was related to the rape victim, he hinted at a conflict of interest on the governor's part. He also mentioned that a favorite ploy of Conlee's, while he was sheriff, had been to call (or pretend to call) the governor's office to impress or intimidate those in *his* office.

Hill sent copies of the letter to "20/20" and *The Commercial Appeal.* Because Hill had mentioned it in his letter, the press picked up on the governor's relation to the rape victim.

One can accuse Clinton of a lot of things, but backward, old-school corruption is not one of them. Perhaps he recognized that he would ignore corrupt politics at his own peril. He swiftly wrote back to Hill, and his response was the lead story in *The Commercial Appeal* under the headline "Letter Stirs Clinton to Order Probe." Clinton asked State Police Director Tommy Goodwin to meet with Hill; the FBI's presence was also requested. The meeting would give Hill a chance to pressure for a more complete probe of the castration.

It was a sunny day in Little Rock. On the picturesque, wooded lot that houses the State Crime Laboratory, the print, radio, and TV reporters milled about. The news trucks were parked nearby.

This was the meeting the governor had ordered. Jack and Anne Hill, who by now were routine subjects of news copy, were coming. Police officials were to be on hand. It was a good story, good for a quick knock-off.

But the reporters got only a superficial account of what happened. Ignoring questions, Jack and Anne marched in—and were quickly deflated. Agent Kelly, the FBI representative who had gotten into the shouting match with Charlie over the Conlee investigation, was there! The meeting was disastrous. Hill was bullied again.

After that, Jack began sinking further into depression. Sure, there had been a few victories here and there, but it seemed as if this episode in his life would drag out forever. He wondered if things would ever change, if Conlee would ever have to answer for what he did.

Later that fall, Anne called Jack from her office. "Are you sitting down?" He was. The results were back, she said. He knew what that meant.

Under the direction of Dumond attorney John Hall, tests on the rape victim's clothing, which still contained residue of the semen from the rape, were conducted. Hall had requested, and received, the clothing in order to conduct genetic allotyping on the semen stains. Despite the age of the stains, all experts said they could still be tested accurately.

Under Hall's direction, Dr. Moses Schanfield, a quiet, soft-spoken scientist who was a top geneticist out of Atlanta, had compared the DNA in the semen to Dumond's DNA, from blood samples. They didn't match. Schanfield said the scientific evidence proved Dumond could not have been the rapist. It happened that quickly—and that slowly. Dumond had finally been cleared of the rape that ruined his life.

Or had he? Even as Arkansas Attorney General Steve Clark remarked that the new evidence "was of tremendous substance. . . . You don't want somebody incarcerated that shouldn't be." Fletcher Long said that while Dumond's attorneys were determined to try Dumond in the press, he would continue to fight it out in court. On November 11, Hall filed a petition with the Arkansas Supreme Court asking for a new trial for Dumond because of the newly discovered evidence. That was a big enough story on its own.

But *The Commercial Appeal* went farther. With Hill's help on sources, the newspaper also made public for the first time Conlee's display of Dumond's testicles:

DUMOND INNOCENT, COURT TOLD
Ex-Sheriff Accused of Bizarre Display

Hill thought that maybe, just maybe, this was the break he had been waiting for. All that work seemed to be paying off. The display of the body parts, which he had known about for years, had finally been made public! And Dumond, it appeared, was an innocent man. The implications were clear. They framed him, they castrated him, they put him away for life. Now they had to do all they could to keep him there.

In prison, an ebullient Dumond held a press conference and said he was a hero to his fellow prisoners. He was getting out, he knew. He had beaten the system; it was just a matter of time. The others looked up to him. He was so sure of it he gave away his Rubik's cube.

Maybe he should have kept it.

In Little Rock, Hall went to the courthouse and filed suit against Conlee for the testicle display, calling it a "tort of outrage . . . conduct which cannot be tolerated in our society." But in St. Francis County, Conlee wasn't finished. He denied everything. He said his political enemies were trying to get him. One of those enemies, he said, was Carl Cisco, the administrator of St. Francis County. Conlee went to the courthouse and filed to run against him.

A few days later, the Arkansas Supreme Court rejected Dumond's request for a circuit court hearing to include details of the genetic testing. The court said that under its post-conviction rules, new evidence wasn't important. In effect, it said Dumond's guilt or innocence didn't matter; what mattered was whether he received a fair trial.

Hill was shocked. This was justice? The courts didn't care that an innocent man was in jail? All that mattered was a technicality? Could this be happening?

By now, though, the publicity mill was working overtime on anything connected to the Dumond case. When Conlee filed a motion asking to dismiss the "tort of outrage" complaint against him for displaying Dumond's testicles, the press was ready to pounce on Hall's court replies. In that court filing, Hall asked: If the testicles were "evidence," as Conlee claimed, why had he seized them with no police record on file? Why did the testicle jar "end up on defendant Conlee's desk?" Why did Conlee treat Dumond's testicles as a "conversation piece or trophy of some sort that he could bring in . . . and then refer to them in euphemistic [street] terms?" Why had Conlee failed to investigate the castration? And if the testicles were of such evidentiary value, "Why were they ceremoniously and ignominiously flushed down the toilet . . . ?"

The testicle case was proving a perfect avenue to attack Conlee on other fronts. Hall asked the federal judge presiding over the case—G. Thomas Eisele—to allow him to introduce evidence that the assailants of Dumond had remarked that "Mr. C. would be proud." And that wasn't all. Hall said, based on Conlee's answers to a series of questions during pretrial discovery, a jury could conclude that the sheriff knew of the castration before it happened. He said, "the jury could infer that defendant Conlee obtained the jar for the testicles before the castration occurred." Although Conlee would give conflicting testimony about that issue, Hall had scored points. The judge didn't allow the "Mr. C." comment on the record, but it was printed in the *Arkansas Democrat*. The jury might not have known, but the state of Arkansas did.

Oscar Fendler, a round, bespectacled, kindly, rambunctious old man, with an Ivy League law degree and a deceivingly friendly nature, was in the twilight of his career when he decided he'd seen enough corruption for one lifetime. One day he decided he would take on the establishment by representing Jack Hill. Fendler criticized Fletcher Long for dropping the assault charges against Calvin Adams, and then it was revealed that Long had served as Adams's personal attorney on another matter (and had failed to inform the court of that fact). Fendler demanded swift litigation of Conlee's libel suit against Hill, a suit that had been left dormant by Conlee but had been hanging over Jack's head, robbing him of job opportunities. Fendler asked for a special prosecutor in East Arkansas, an independent authority who could look into official corruption. "You'll have to hold your nose if you get within ten miles of Forrest City," he would tell the state supreme court in one oral argument.

Fendler set an angry, combative tone, but that might be expected of one of the few Jews to grow up in Northeast Arkansas, the kind who'd slip off to Klan meetings to learn more about the rednecks he was dealing with. The moves put Hill back on the offensive for the first time in years. Though Jack had sunk to new lows of personal despair, publicly he had kept a stiff upper lip. Now it wasn't just an act. He could walk tall again.

All in all, it wasn't a good month for Fletcher Long. After absorbing Fendler's broadsides, he was subpoenaed to testify before the grand jury that was investigating Conlee. During one unpleasant afternoon, Long was chased by a bunch of Little Rock reporters and "20/20" 's Thompson as he ducked out of the federal courthouse. They caught him. He didn't have much comment.

From his network of St. Francis County sources, Hill got wind of the topics of the federal probe. The mysterious fire at Forrest City Aviation, the suspected arson that, perhaps more than anything else, had led Hill down this path, was at the top of the list. With Fendler's help (his constant pushing for action on the libel suit) Jack got a copy of the state police file on the Forrest City Aviation fire. He released it to *The Commercial Appeal,* and a motive surfaced: the newspaper reported the file's conclusion that Conlee had been losing between $10,000 and $12,000 a month on the business when it burned. Also, Sambo Hughes, Conlee's chief deputy, admitted he'd bought three cans of lighter fluid from a convenience store, another fact uncovered by Hill and now public knowledge.

But Hill still could not breathe more easily. Though the tide seemed to be turning, he knew the fight wasn't over. Dumond was still in prison—and so was Jack; he was still a prisoner to the story. He had been isolated from his own profession, severed from his livelihood and the job he loved.

Twenty

For if a democracy is to function, the voters surely have
a right to know as much as they decently can about the
men and women who govern them.

—Arthur Schlesinger

By March in the Delta, winter is always over. The sun comes
out early and bright, bringing with it the farmers to the
fields. In 1988, that coming spring brought the wind of
change.

The people were opening their eyes. Black attorneys,
still few in number, were speaking out. Bill Lewellen had
won a crucial victory over Raff for racially motivated prosecution. Olly Neal was willing to stand up for what he believed to be right. Still others decried Raff publicly, something that had never happened before.

One of those men with a good conscience was Dan Dane, a brash, mustachioed, white attorney in Forrest City, who became appalled at the crime in the streets and the deterioration of his community. A native Missourian, he had moved to Arkansas as an admirer of the state's rustic wildlife and rugged scenery. But when he looked around Forrest City, he saw none of the quaint innocence that had attracted him in the beginning. Instead he saw drugs on the streets, kids with guns, arsons gone unpunished, people being murdered in their homes.

On a winter day, Dane, now gaining in maturity and status, was approached in his office by a handful of attorneys, who secretly confided to him that they wanted him to run for prosecutor against Raff in the early spring primary. It was something no one had ever done before. But now Dan Dane felt the tug of his peers, the call of destiny, and he could no longer turn his back.

While Dane was preparing to enter politics for the first time, Coolidge was already running again. He had always wanted to be county judge in St. Francis County, the elected administrative office that had nothing to do with being a judge. The county judge was a patron of the county who was executive officer of the quorum court, the county council. Conlee had always wanted to teach incumbent Carl Cisco a lesson.

Many thought Conlee could win in 1988, despite the federal probe of him and the bad publicity that had come out. The testicle case was a little bit of baggage, to be sure, but Coolidge thought he could overcome it. Hell, he'd just had a little fun at the expense of a convicted rapist. But of course, he didn't say that publicly. He just denied it happened. "Street talk," he called it.

*   *   *

Both races were as tough as Arkansas had ever seen.

Dane ran on the claim that "a climate of lawlessness" pervaded St. Francis County and the Delta. He painted a portrait of an outlaw flatlands that had gone out of control. The "failure of the prosecuting attorney" to do his job was to blame, Dane said. He was particularly upset about Raff's record on drug convictions. He noted that, in St. Francis County, of twenty-seven drug-related felony cases he examined, twenty-four were never prosecuted; two were reduced to misdemeanors, and only one person was convicted. When news reports were circulated about this, Raff was unavailable for comment,

There was more bad news for Raff during the campaign. *The Commercial Appeal* broke the story that Raff, a member of the State Police Commission and an elected prosecutor, had been sworn in as a deputy sheriff in Phillips County, his home base. Attorney General Steve Clark told the newspaper that it was against the law for a lawyer to serve as a sheriff in any jurisdiction where he practiced law. That hurt Raff. At a press conference, somebody asked Clinton how he could allow a man whom he had appointed to the State Police Commission to continue to serve on the commission when he had violated the law.

"I was told that he didn't know that it was against the law," Clinton said.

"Who told you that?" the reporter wondered.

"I don't remember," the governor shot back. The explanation was so pat it didn't ring true. But there was no real way to challenge it. Raff stayed on the commission.

The campaign for prosecutor was nasty, but Raff left

much of his campaigning up to his deputies, including Long. Long was able to provide some of the blistering replies to Dane's charges, sneering at Dane's inexperience in dealing with real-life cases. Dane hinted he feared for his safety. He kept a gun close at hand. His backers said they were worried about vote fraud.

And that was just the half of it. In St. Francis County, in his race for county judge, Coolidge was distributing pamphlets saying incumbent Cisco had brought on all of St. Francis County's bad publicity by being one of Jack Hill's informants. Coolidge also accused Cisco of using county funds for private favors.

Then there was the business Coolidge brought up about Cisco's sexual preferences, that he supposedly had a thing for black women. In the Delta, such a charge could prove disastrous to a man like Cisco, who is white.

Conlee made one of his stump speeches in a seedy, dark funeral home for blacks. The lime-green carpets, punctured with cigarette burns, led into a back-room chapel. A group of black ministers held a serious meeting to discuss Cisco's supposed sex crimes. An older black man, looking sad and uncomfortable, told the ministers Cisco had propositioned his daughter. Deputy prosecutor Long gave them a donation, and on the altar, Coolidge gave them a quick, drawling speech to say that only he could return "morality" to the county judge's office.

Few remember it now, but Clinton came within an eyelash of running for president in 1988. He backed out at the last moment, saying he was concerned what a campaign would do to his daughter, Chelsea. So the mantle of Southern candidate was worn by another man that year—Al Gore, Jr.

On March 8, 1988, while the nation was watching the victories of the Southern presidential candidate in the South's "Super Tuesday" presidential primaries, Anne Hill spent the day in anticipation of Southern election results that told the real story of how the region's political views had evolved since the Vietnam War. And this time, unlike in 1986 when Parkman had eked out a win over Conlee, it didn't take all night to learn who would win in East Arkansas. In Dan Dane's Forrest City office, Anne watched as Dane's friends began slapping him on the back early in the evening. Both Raff and Conlee were overwhelmingly defeated in their primary elections. Raff carried only one county in the six-county district, and Conlee lost by an even wider margin in St. Francis County.

Raff and his cohorts were to leave power at the end of the year, and the First Judicial District had begun to close the door on an era that Dane would later say it should never forget.

Twenty-One

There is no way that Mr. Dumond could have donated that semen.

—Moses Schanfield, Atlanta geneticist

Wayne Dumond finally made it back to St. Francis County, not that he ever really wanted to. The Arkansas Supreme Court ordered a hearing for Dumond, the first time that it had ever given him any kind of postconviction relief. But it wasn't supposed to be on the new genetic evidence. Instead, the court said it was concerned that a mistrial motion may have been made and gone unrecorded by Dumond's original trial attorneys. It ordered a lower court to find out whether the motion had been made. The higher court would determine whether any of it really mattered.

Dumond, still a state prisoner, was led into the same

St. Francis County courtroom where he had been convicted, in the same courthouse where his testicles had been put on display. Raff was there. Long was there. Only this time it was the press that filled the jury box. Local television crews were on hand, as were the big network cameras for "20/20."

Dr. Moses Schanfield, who had performed the new genetic tests on the semen stains on the rape victim's clothing, said that his tests, called immunoglobulin allotyping, focused on surface proteins carried throughout the bodily fluids. He said simply that the DNA from the semen did not match Dumond's DNA.

"There is no way that Mr. Dumond could have donated that semen," he said. But under tough, skilled cross-examination by Long, Schanfield said the tests weren't infallible. After all, he said, nothing was infallible.

Long called the testing "witchcraft." He told the press, "We've got people playing games with the system of justice—'20/20' news." He said "20/20" "had no story" unless it could prove Dumond innocent. Charlie Thompson, ever the calm, subtle network producer, replied, "He's just a crybaby."

The judge sent a transcript of the proceedings back to the state supreme court. Hall nearly laughed at the way the matter was being handled. "It doesn't matter that you're innocent," he said. "It's form over substance."

Outside this public play, Dusty and Wayne married again in Forrest City. The divorce for financial reasons was over. She was married to a convict again.

For Jack, all the manipulations provided little solace as he sank more deeply into financial insolvency. He was forced to take a job in telemarketing. It was humiliating, pressuring people to buy something they didn't need, and Jack wasn't very good at it. He was too honest.

Together Anne and Jack were living day-to-day. He figured the whole episode, including lost earnings, savings, and the house, had cost him $250,000. He was wondering how much longer the Buick would hold out.

He prayed.

Conlee was finished politically, but Anne deeply believed that wasn't punishment enough. So she and ABC's Thompson spent hours in the federal court building in Little Rock, where the federal grand jury was looking into the high crimes of the high sheriff.

The characters of St. Francis County, whom they had gotten to know so well over the years—the characters in Christian's diary, came to life and one-by-one walked past Anne and Charlie into the closed grand-jury room: Conlee's cronies, black nightclub owners, those who knew about arsons-for-profit, drug dealers who said the sheriff had given them reduced sentences in exchange for payoffs, and people who'd bought their way out of jail.

But despite Thompson's pressures, the investigation dragged on, and forever it seemed as if there would be no indictments.

Finally, May came. Jack Hill was at his lowly telemarketing job that afternoon. It was a Tuesday. He'd heard that maybe—just maybe—the indictments would be handed down that day.

He took a break from the telephone sales pitches to catch the 6 o'clock news. But the barber shop next door was closed.

He saw a TV set in a nearby paramedic's office. The door was locked, and he couldn't hear anything. But he would know whether the indictments had come down if they just showed Conlee's face on the news. He approached the window. He waited through a commercial. But then he laughed at himself. The set was tuned to MTV.

He couldn't call Anne. She was at the courthouse. He would just have to wait.

That night, he got home and finally caught the late news.

It had been a mad scene at the federal building. A crush of reporters pressed together. Word was, something was coming down. Body odor wafted through the hallway press conference. The television lights were hot and blinding, bringing out sweat. The microphones were thrust forward like torches. United States Attorney Chuck Banks emerged from his office and stood outside the federal courtrooms. The cameras rolled.

He read a statement in a steady voice: Coolidge Conlee, deputy Sambo Hughes, and Forrest City bail bondsman Danny Burns had been indicted on charges of racketeering, drug dealing, arson, mail fraud, extortion, and gambling.

Hill rejoiced when he saw it on the news. There were twenty-seven counts! The charge was that Conlee and friends "operated the St. Francis County Sheriff's Office as a conduit to obtain monetary benefits to themselves and associated entities and to participate in and conceal their illegal activities."

The drug case that Hill made public at KAIT was the first charge. The extortion charge was based on the "shakedown" of black nightclub owners, who were forced to make monthly payments to Hughes and Conlee to stay open. The gambling charge linked the men to high-stakes crap shoots in the sheriff's office. The arson and mail fraud charges were linked to the fire at Forrest City Aviation.

Conlee had a heavy load to bear. He was charged with two counts of extortion, one count of conspiracy to distribute marijuana, one count of arson, and sixteen counts of mail fraud.

Shortly after the indictments were handed down, Conlee's attorney, Mike Easley of Forrest City, faced the press to deny the charges. He said the former sheriff was the victim of a vendetta perpetrated by Jack Hill and federal authorities and that the press "obviously enjoyed" the opportunity to go after a public figure. He vowed to take the case to trial.

The press conference didn't end in the federal building. Reporters called Jack Hill for reaction. He was only too happy to oblige. He was happy, but an indictment wasn't a conviction. He had almost won.

But not quite.

Twenty-Two

Evidence obtained after a conviction is not a basis for
postconviction relief.

—The Arkansas Supreme Court

In Cummins the prisoners don't do much celebrating, no
matter what the news; so Dumond didn't react much when
he heard of Conlee's indictment. In prison he had more mundane things to deal with, such as protecting himself from
coercion and attack. The fact that there were gay men on
the make in prison wasn't really the problem. On that subject
he would remark: "There's plenty of that goin' on. But I do
not indulge." He had a choice about gays, he said, because
nobody tried to force him. But he was worried about the
toughs, the guys who tried to be boss.

To deal with them, Dumond had cultivated his image

as a crazy man. After a while, nobody wanted to mess with him. That was for the best. He would tell a visitor that he wasn't afraid to do what he had to do.

> Yeah, it's true. I have gotten to the point where, if somebody wanted to vent somethin' on me, I would do what I had to do. If that meant killin' him, I'd have to kill him. I don't look for trouble. Never have looked for trouble. But that wouldn't stop me.

While he was under indictment, Conlee was arrested for running a gambling house at Forrest City Ready Mix. Nobody was particularly surprised at the charges; Conlee and the owner were accused of running a high-stakes game. Sheriff Dave Parkman sent a warning through the county: "I will not tolerate high-stakes gambling—and I'd like to underline high-stakes—in our county."

Hill just shook his head. Conlee's arrogance was unequaled! While he was under indictment, he went right on doing the same old things. Would he never learn?

About this time, a cloud that had hung over Jack Hill's head for more than two years lifted. Conlee dropped the libel suit. Fendler's tactics of pushing for action on the suit had worked. Conlee was cowed into backing down.

Of course, Michael Easley's court filing, which withdrew the suit, virtually libeled Hill. He said Jack had launched a "personal vendetta" against Conlee, "apparently due to Hill's long-term unemployment."

> Hill's unemployment results from his habit of compulsive and obsessive behavior in investigating this story and in

failing to report the news objectively.

It is obvious that those media sources whom Hill has approached for a job recognize the danger in hiring this "loose cannon" and have declined to employ him. . . .

[Conlee] does not wish to subject himself to unscrupulous, scandalous and dishonest publicity stunts such as the one perpetrated by Oscar Fendler and Jack Hill. . . .

It had never really occurred to Hill, but maybe there was some truth in the notion that he'd been blackballed from his own profession. If so, he saw more than a little irony in the fact that the blackballing had come about because he championed the very things that journalists claimed they held dear—the fight for justice, the aggressive monitoring of corrupt public officials, the First Amendment.

Following the hearing in Forrest City, it didn't take long for the Arkansas Supreme Court to toss aside, once again, any notion that it might consider the genetic evidence in deciding whether Dumond should be granted a new trial. With its feet firmly in concrete, it noted that "evidence obtained after a conviction is not a basis for postconviction relief" under its rules.

Hall wasn't surprised. "Guilt or innocence doesn't have anything to do with whether you get a new trial in Arkansas," he remarked.

As Dumond was still fighting and losing his battles, Conlee was waging his own war. The attorneys for the sheriff, Sambo Hughes and Danny Burns tried claiming that the FBI investigation in St. Francis County amounted to a "reign of terror." Conlee and Burns said the indictment was "based solely upon the accusations contained in a series of 'investigative reports' by a publicity-seeking journalist from Jonesboro." Burns said he was offered a bribe by the FBI to testify against Conlee.

But Assistant U.S. Attorney Michael Johnson, who was to help prosecute the case, told the court: "The defendants have gone too far. . . . They have made these allegations with reckless disregard for their veracity. The freedom to criticize the government is not a carte blanche for falsehood."

After a hearing, Judge Eisele ruled that the defendants' charges had no basis. He said the government might have been rude or heavy-handed, but there was no evidence of impropriety. His ruling cleared the way for the U.S. government to try Conlee.

But before that, Conlee had another trial to face. He had to answer for his fun-house display of Wayne Dumond's testicles.

Twenty-Three

You'd have to know what you was looking for to know
that they was his testicles. There was so much blood in
there.

—Coolidge Conlee

The air-conditioning wasn't working in the United States
District Court on August 15, 1988, when court convened
for Wayne Dumond's lawsuit against Coolidge Conlee and
St. Francis County. Spectators and jurors were sweaty and
faint. Judge G. Thomas Eisele (pronounced EYES-lee) repeatedly cut the hours short and implored technicians to
do something about the air-conditioning. But it didn't do
much good. Throughout the trial, there was no respite.

Perhaps the stifling oppressiveness was appropriate for
Dumond's "tort of outrage" claims. The suit was based on
a charge that Conlee, by showing off Dumond's testicles,

199

had committed a reprehensible act so beyond the bounds
of ordinary conduct that it damaged Dumond and deserved
civil punishment.

Eisele, an owlish, scholarly, white-haired judge with
glasses and thick, almost cartoonish white eyebrows, pre-
sided as Dumond's attorney, Hall, and the attorney for Conlee, Bob Roddy, squared off. Roddy's main task was to protect
the county and the insurance company, for Conlee didn't
have any money. If Dumond won, it would be the county's
insurance company that would pay.

Meanwhile, the deliberate Hall had prepared for the case
with the argument that Dumond and his family had been
irreparably harmed by Conlee's ghoulish display of the body
parts. Hall brought forth all the witnesses—Wayne, Dusty,
Marcy Halbert, O'Neal Webb. Regan Hill, from the funeral
home owned by the father, testified about the presence of
the sheriff and the testicles at the funeral home. The father
of the victim testified, and, by deposition, so did an FBI
agent by the name of Charles Williams, who said he had
been called into Conlee's office and shown Dumond's
testicles.

The testimony was unlike any ever before heard in a
U.S. federal court. To set up for the jury what had happened,
Hall called Wayne Dumond to the witness stand first. Dumond had traveled from Cummins prison, in South Arkansas,
to appear in court. Under questioning from Hall, Dumond
said he watched "All My Children" the day he was castrated,
then the noon news. He made a couple of drinks, Jim Beam
and Coke. After he got the mail, two men burst in the front
door. The taller man wore a dark turtleneck, dark slacks,
and cowboy boots. The shorter had on a western-style shirt
and blue jeans. One of them put a .38 revolver to his head.

The little fellow, he had a hold of my hair. He kept pulling on my hair and keeping that gun right there. He had the gun up here to my temple. I'm worried about the gun going off and I'm worried about what this other guy is doing. He's tying me up and then he—it really shocked me when he started to pull my trousers down. I'm screaming and begging: "What are you guys doing? What do you want? Please don't do this!"

And the fellow, he produced a little knife. I want to say it was a hunting knife. Had about a three-inch blade on it—wide blade.

Hall asked, "They cut you?"

"Twice," said Dumond. He said he knew what had happened, that they had castrated him. He wriggled around, trying to get loose, but realized it was doing no good. He waited, bleeding.

Later, Dumond said he was told by his attorney and others that "the testicles had been put in a jar and had been preserved and that Mr. Conlee was allegedly displaying those testicles down in his office. And this horrified me. I said, 'This is wrong. What this man is doing is wrong.' It scared me."

"Why did it scare you?" Hall asked.

I had already been attacked, came close to expiration, I think. And here this man is going to be atrocious enough to show severed body parts to people around town. I mean, it's bad enough that I had to be accused of a crime that I didn't commit, but to have the man to humiliate me that way by showing these parts—these private body parts, not a hand or a finger, but those private body parts, testicles. . . . It was more than I could take. Me and my family left Forrest City. We went to DeWitt and stayed.

Dumond said his emotions slowly changed from humiliation to anger. "I am mad. I mean, he didn't have no right to do that."

Hall asked him, "How do you feel about today having to testify about what happened to you on March 7?"

"The only thing good about today is the fact I got away from Cummins for one day. That's the only thing good about it."

Dumond said he was outraged that the testicles were eventually just flushed down the toilet.

> I'd of liked to had them back for my own—I could have got rid of them. I could have buried them. I could have flushed them down the toilet, you know, if I would have wanted to. They were mine. Those were my testicles. He didn't have no right to take them and he didn't have no right to show them around and he didn't have no right to flush them down the toilet.

Still under oath, Dumond tried to explain why these events caused him to be suicidal, why he felt he'd been damaged by the sheriff's actions:

> I can't single out—there's night after night after night that I lay there. I go to bed at 10 o'clock every night [in prison]. I turn back the covers and get in bed at 10 o'clock because I have to get up early. There's many a night goes by when I watch the clock way past midnight just thinking about everything. I can't sit there and tell you it's because of this, because Coolidge Conlee displayed my severed body parts that I can't sleep. I can't tell you that. It's everything combined: being charged with something I didn't do, being attacked the way I was attacked, things that happened to

me since I've been here, the fear of whether or not I'm going
to get out of here, will justice ever be done for me or am
I going to have to spend the rest of my life in the penitentiary?
It's all of that combined, Mister, that makes me want to
go all the way off and do something really crazy.

Next, Hall called Dusty, who recounted Wayne's horror
at learning of the castration and Conlee's display of the
testicles. She stared straight at Hall as she spoke.

Well, it about destroyed him, the self-confidence he had.
The accusation he castrated himself was bad. The fact
that he suffered through the terrible suffering of being
mutilated like that, an intentional murder planned, to think
that his name was destroyed and put on a bottle that had
his very private parts to be passed around with the sheriff
proud of his trophies, I just—it was almost more than
he could stand or any of us to see him suffer so.
   He cried. He had breakdowns. When we found out
the sheriff had his testicles in a jar, we felt that maybe
the sheriff would put my breast in a jar. We didn't know
what he would plan next, so that was one of the things
that made us decide to go into hiding. We didn't know
what was ahead of us if we stayed.

The third family member to testify was Michael Dumond,
Dumond's son, fourteen at the time, who had found his father
bound and bleeding. By now it was clear that Hall was slowly
building a case to show how all the circumstances had devas-
tated the Dumond family. Michael's testimony was short,
but poignant.
Hall asked Michael:

Would you tell the court and the jury about the day you came home from school and found your father at home and what you saw?

When we was walking in and we was in the kitchen and I saw him there laying in a puddle of blood.

How were his hands?

Tied behind his back.

And his feet?

Tied behind his back.

Could you tell where he had been cut?

No.

What did you do when you found him?

I cut him loose.

Where did you get the knife?

Out of the drawer in the kitchen.

Did somebody go for help?

My little brother.

What was his name?

Joey.

And how old was he back then?

Nine.

Hall then asked Michael if he knew anything about first aid to help his father.
"No."

Hall said, "When did you find out what happened to your dad?"

Michael replied softly, "A few nights later on the news."

Then it was time for the sheriff to testify. He slowly stepped foward, was sworn in, and sat down gingerly.

As a way of introduction, Hall asked Conlee to summarize his career.

"I was elected to City Council in '72 and served on it for two years, and then I was elected mayor of Forrest City in '74 and served as mayor for six years. Then I was elected sheriff in '80 and served six years as sheriff of St. Francis County."

"And in 1986 you were defeated for re-election?" Hall asked him.

"I seeked re-election and got beat."

When Hall asked him to describe his career before he sought public office in St. Francis County, the sheriff said:

Well, during the race meet of '60, I'd go to Hot Springs and work in Hot Springs at the Vapors or the Belvedere in the race meet. Then I'd come back home and work for Twenty-One Club there for about a year and a half. . . . In 1963 I'd got out of the club business and moved back to Hot Springs and started working over there until 1967. And when Rockefeller vetoed the gambling bill, I came home and went into heavy construction. That's heavy equipment: building roads, streets, clearing land and stuff like that.

Then Hall turned to the day in question, March 7, 1985, when Dumond was castrated. Conlee said his criminal investigator, Chuck Thomas, was already at the scene when he arrived.

And so I got out and Chuck had already been in the house and he said, "Well, come on in here. I have got something I don't know what to do with."

So we went in there and how horrible it was and everything. And so, he got the—well, first he said something about, "Well, let's pick up the whiskey bottle." There was a half-gallon whiskey bottle on the table there. . . .

But while he was there he taken some pictures and so from the living room—what I call the living room, going up the steps going into the kitchen back to the phone there, you could see somone had drug hisself back to this phone and got the phone off the hook and it was still off the hook. And I picked up—

"There wasn't anybody in the house at that time, was there?" Hall interrupted.

Beg your pardon?

There wasn't anybody in the house that belonged to that blood, was there?

No, sir. . . . And the best as I can recall, east of where the phone was hanging on the wall there is a bed there. And there was a billfold on the bed and I got out the billfold, reached in there and I got his driver's license out. It said, "Wayne Dumond." And we didn't even know who it was at first. And they said, "Wayne Dumond."

Conlee said he and Thomas then went to the emergency room to see Dumond. From the hospital, Conlee said he called State Police investigator Phil Osterman.

At that point did you know what had happened to Wayne Dumond?

No, sir. At that particular point I didn't. The only thing I know is what the doctor made the remark. . . . "Well, I've got the blood stopped." Said, "I've got the blood stopped." And that's when I crept on out the back.

At that point did you know he'd been castrated?

I want to say—yeah, I believe I did know he was castrated.

And you were in the house and looked around the inside of the house, did you not?

Yes, sir. Yes, sir.

And his testicles were, in fact, on the floor in the house, weren't they?

Yeah, but they was all in blood. You'd have to know what you was looking for to know that they was his testicles. There was so much blood in there.

And did you know—did you see his testicles on the floor there at that time?

I didn't know that they were his testicles on the floor there at that time.

Hall kept at him. What did Conlee know and when did he know it? It was a crucial issue. But even Conlee wasn't clear.
Hall asked him:

When you first got there you didn't know what you had?

That's right.

But you had determined that he'd been castrated?

I had determined it.

And you couldn't tell that that was his testicles on the floor?

Well, I mean, I didn't know whether he was castrated or not.

When you got to the hospital you told Dusty Dumond that her husband had been castrated, didn't you?

I just—whatever Dr. Meredith—he come out of the office—I mean out of the emergency room and he made the remark about—about—Meredith made the remark about Wayne Dumond being castrated and he said, "I've got the blood stopped."

So the doctor mentioned it, then?

Yes, sir.

After Osterman, Conlee, and Forrest City police officer Stacy Dye went back out to Dumond's house, the sheriff testified, he told Dye to check the serial numbers on Dumond's guns. Then he testified Osterman ordered that the serial numbers be checked; then he said again that he had asked that the numbers be checked. He also said Osterman ordered everything—the twine used to bind Dumond, the testicles, everything—to be picked up.

Of course, it was easy for Conlee to put words in Osterman's mouth without fear of contradiction. Osterman had been killed in a plane crash some months earlier. However, Osterman had described to others how Conlee had seemed obsessed with the testicles, and how the sheriff had taken it upon himself to step into the blood and pick them up.

Here's Conlee's version:

> So we—I got a little old match box—oh, it was, I guess,
> about that long that you buy these matches in—you buy
> fifty in a box. And one of them little old boxes was down
> there by the wall there, so I started putting the strings
> in it and—the ones I could touch without getting hold of
> blood and it was a ball of twine you could see was down
> in a clot of blood and I wasn't aiming to pick it up.
>
> I said, "Well, Phil, I'm not going to get this here." He
> said, "Yeah, we have got to get everything." And about
> that time it was a pair, looked like, of doctor's scissors—
> oh, they was about that long—laying on this same—the
> same top that the paring knife was on. . . . They was about
> that long and they was surgical scissors. He handed them
> to me and says, "See if you can get them with that."
>
> So I taken the end of them and started getting them,
> started putting them in a sack, getting them on down. I
> had trouble getting it around that ball but I finally got
> it around that ball and throwed it in there. . . .
>
> And so, about that time Phil said, "I'm going to go
> outside and look for tracks and see if I can find any tracks
> out around here." So he had his flashlight and just as he
> passed by I noticed something down there. I said, "This
> is human down here." He said, "I want everything. Put
> it in the box."
>
> And I put it in the box. It was his testicles.

Perhaps that was the moment when the walls really
crumbled around Coolidge Conlee. In open court, in front
of a jury and a studious, rather stern judge, by his own
words, he had picked up another man's testicles in order

to save them. Yet Conlee, oblivious to it all, just kept chattering. He thought he had a perfect excuse: A dead man had told him to do it.

Later, Hall went back to the testicles.

And what about the testicles? Where were they?

They was in a little old—like I say, the matchbox that you buy fifty matches in at the store. I don't know what you call them. The matches here you take one of them out and use it and—it wasn't no box of matches. It was just open—like you have them open-type matches. Book matches, they call them.

He said he carried the testicles outside to the car and put them in the back on the floorboard, beside the other evidence. But he knew he had to preserve them because, Conlee testified, Osterman told him, "I want you to put them testicles in some alcohol." So he said he called the state medical examiner, Fahmy Malak, and asked him, "What would you put testicles in?" It was Malak who told him to use formaldehyde, the sheriff said.

Conlee said he tried to go to the Palace Drug Store for pure grain alcohol or formaldehyde, but it was night now and the store was closed. So he started to go to Safeway, a grocery store, or to Wal-Mart, "but I happened to think I had to have me a jar to get them in. That's whenever— I live on the second hill from Palace Drug Store and that's where it came to me after—I said I could have picked a jar up at . . . [the funeral home owned by the rape victim's father]. When I left there, I went straight home and got a quart jar and went down to . . . [the funeral home]."

The sheriff met funeral home employee Regan Hill, whom

he had called from home, at the mortuary. He said the victim's father was also at the funeral home.

> When I got out of the car I put the—I got the jar at home, I put it right back there in the back seat with the rest of it. When I got out of the car there at the funeral home, I taken the box, taken the lid off the thing and dumped them over in this quart fruit jar and put the box back in there in the car and went in there with the jar.

After Regan Hill poured formaldehyde over the testicles, the sheriff left the funeral home. He said he then took the victim's father back to the steak dinner the father had been attending that night.

Hall asked him:

And did you and . . . [the father] talk about the castration?

No, sir, we did not mention it.

And you had the jar in the back seat, though?

Yes, sir, I had it right behind me in the back seat.

And you knew that the jar in the back seat had the testicles that belonged to the man that was accused of raping that man's daughter?

Well, he was accused of it, yeah.

And you never mentioned it to him?

No, sir. No, sir.

Conlee said he tried to find Osterman again that night, but couldn't. In fact, it was kind of funny. The sheriff said that Osterman—who according to Conlee ordered the preservation of all the evidence, including the testicles—never came to pick up any of it. So Conlee, poor Conlee, was left holding the stuff.

He took advantage of this opportunity. The next day, Conlee ran into clerk Bill Gatlin, who swore the sheriff showed him the testicles as he was coming into the courthouse. Conlee said no, he just told Gatlin he had a lot of evidence. Conlee said he put the jar inside the evidence vault, which wasn't locked, "and I caught a lot of people—observed a lot of people over there looking—sticking around in that—looking in the vault."

So, the sheriff said, he had to get the testicles away from all these curiosity-seekers. So he put the jar behind him, he said, and trying to explain, said, "My desk was like this, and I had a little hammock thing . . . a little kanacki—what do you call it?—that you can store stuff. It's a metal thing; it's got sliding doors."

"Credenza, you mean?" Hall asked him.

"Yeah, uh-huh, that's what it was." He said a bunch of people came up to his office wanting to see the testicles, so that's why he kept them where he could keep track of them.

Conlee said he showed the testicles only to other law enforcement authorities, including Osterman and FBI men Scottie Battershell and Charles Williams. (Williams later would say he was "dumbfounded" as to why the sheriff showed him the body parts.) But he never showed the testicles to anyone else, he said.

Hall concluded his examination of Conlee by noting that Conlee, in a sworn deposition, had said he got the jar for the testicles at the funeral home. Yet in court, Conlee said he got the jar at home. Under cross-examination, Conlee said his memory was faulty when he said the jar was from the funeral home.

Under cross-examination, Conlee also elaborated on his answer about the doctor telling him that Dumond was castrated: "Whenever the doctor and all of us walked out in the hall out there, he says, 'I got the blood stopped. And I asked him, 'How did you do that?' He says, 'Crammed towels up in there.' And he says, 'He sure was castrated.' "

Boy, he sure was.

Federal agents would joke later that it was a "balls-out case." The evidence was to include photographs of the crime scene, a bloody mess of a kitchen floor—with Dumond's testicles in the pool of blood. And the parade of witnesses that followed made Conlee look like a liar. Marcy Halbert told about her experience with the testicles. So did O'Neal Webb. So did the father of the victim, in a deposition. He testified that he went back to the funeral home the night Conlee had the testicles because his wife reached him at the steak supper and told him the sheriff's office was trying to reach him. After checking at the courthouse for Conlee, the father was told the sheriff was at the funeral home. Conlee, the father told him, had needed formaldehyde for the testicles. About all that was said between them, the father testified, was that Conlee said, " 'Here are Dumond's testicles. Do you want to see them?' Of course, they are looking at me, so that was it."

Hall's closing arguments were blunt. He said simply that the testicle display was the "ultimate insult," and asked jurors to send a signal that such behavior could not be tolerated.

*   *   *

The jurors went out for about an hour and a half. There really hadn't been much doubt about the evidence. The question was whether Conlee's actions were egregious enough to warrant a penalty.

But the jury gave a resounding answer. In answers to court "interrogatories"—questions designed to help a jury deliberate—the jury found that Conlee's conduct was an arbitrary police intrusion into Dumond's privacy. The jury also found that the action was "so inspired by ill will or malice rather than being done merely through carelessness that it amounted to an inhumane abuse of official power literally shocking to the conscience."

After that it was merely a matter of setting damages. The jury gave Dumond $100,000 in compensatory damages, and $50,000 in punitive damages.

Conlee was stunned. But it didn't really hurt him personally. After all, he had been sheriff, and his actions had been insured. Hall later said he "gave them a discount" for not appealing the verdict, and the eventual payment to Dumond was about $100,000.

In a footnote to the testicle case, the *Arkansas Democrat* noted in an editorial that the verdict was "justice of a sort." It went on to say the display showed a "sick sense of humor. Such an act is an outrage not only against Wayne Dumond, but an outrage against every civilized human being in Arkansas. To think Conlee was once a county sheriff, a trusted servant of the people and guardian of their safety, makes the blood run cold."

*   *   *

At the same time, Dumond finally lost his last appeal in state courts. The Arkansas Supreme Court rejected all his arguments for a new trial. Hill mused that the justices may not have realized it, but the ruling had the effect of elevating Dumond from being just another prisoner, another loser. Now he had become a political prisoner; now he was a symbol of the moss-backed mentality of public officials who kept the South on the bottom.

It was an institutional failure of the worst kind, Hill believed. It put the spotlight on the type of men who could not look past narrow technicalities to see a larger truth. The chilling reality to Hill was: if an innocent Wayne Dumond could be imprisoned, then no one was safe.

Twenty-Four

I can't for the life of me figure out why they brought this case to trial, except they got a Judas to sell out.

—Mike Easley

. . . and you will know the truth, and the truth will make you free.

—John 8:32

For a long time he lived in 19 Barracks, with dozens of others. He became a tutor because he was literate and many of his cohorts were not. Dumond taught his fellow prisoners how to read.

He took showers in groups, with a stall. Occasionally, he got a few comments about what was missing down below.

He would remark:

Only those that know me well enough know that they can joke about it. Joe Fountain is one of them. He's pure convict. He gets along with everybody, but he's real suave about it. He claims to have two real friends in the penitentiary. And I'm one of them. I've got a book that I keep people's quaint little sayin's, and he wrote me a letter in this book. And he called me his brother. "If you ever need anything, you holler, and you'll get it."

Then the case against Conlee broke. It was unexpected at the time, but for the government, it made perfect sense. Sambo Hughes and Danny Burns agreed to plead guilty and testify against their former crony Coolidge Conlee. They wouldn't lie for a liar.

It was devastating. The world had come crashing down on Conlee. The government quickly moved to streamline its case by going to its heart. It dropped the drug charges and the charges related to the fire at Forrest City Aviation.

In his guilty plea, Hughes said he extorted $100 to $200 every week from three black nightclub owners for at least two years. In return, they were allowed to run their gambling parlors. Burns pleaded guilty to a misdemeanor marijuana possession charge.

Hughes faced a maximum penalty of twenty years in prison and a fine of $250,000. Burns faced a fine of up to $100,000 and less than a year in jail. Their new possible jail time was nothing compared to what they had faced. Hughes could have been sent away for more than two hundred years.

Mr. C. would stand trial alone.

Easley was outraged. "This is horrible," he said. The whole thing "stinks"; it wasn't fair, he said.

Tough. The grand jury revised the charges against Conlee. On Halloween, he was named in an eight-count indictment for racketeering, extortion, and gambling. He was scheduled to stand trial the next day. Specifically, the charges were stiff. Conlee was accused of receiving $1,500 as a bribe to reduce a felony charge of manufacturing marijuana to a misdemeanor; of extorting $3,000 from a nightclub owner to reduce a felony charge of operating a gambling house; of extorting at least $100 a week from five nightclub owners; and of misusing the sheriff's office to engage in racketeering and gambling.

As he entered the Little Rock courtroom, Conlee knew the stakes. He faced one hundred and sixty years in jail. Presiding was the scowling Judge Eisele, the same judge who had sat on the testicle case.

The witnesses nailed Conlee.

Roy Akers, a former deputy and jailer, told about dice games in the sheriff's office, even while black club operator Dan Malone of Hicks Station was arrested for running a gambling house. But he said Sambo Hughes told him to back off people like Malone.

Carolyn Searcy, who handled collections for the sheriff, said Conlee gave her a gold necklace and offered to give her a car from his used car lot for "a little consideration." She also said he suggested a trip to Las Vegas. She paid for the car and turned down the trip.

Charles Lee told of having to pay the sheriff's office $3,000 to get out of a marijuana charge. Constable Robert Smith told about his famous $1,200 roll of the dice in the sheriff's office. Marcy Halbert told about rolling dice for $20 a bet.

It was piling on.

Dora Flanagin Hughes struck some courtroom observers as a little batty, but her testimony clearly hurt Conlee. Here was the sister of the local state representative, the wife of Conlee's chief deputy—former Conlee allies all—talking about rolling dice in the sheriff's office. She said Conlee once financed a dice roll for her and profited by $350 when she won.

She wasn't happy to be there, but she was on her husband Sambo's side now, and Easley couldn't shake her. When Easley tried to downplay the crap shoots, implying they were just fun and games, Dora shot back, "Why am I sitting here embarrassing myself saying this if we haven't done something wrong?" The courtroom broke up. Easley just moved on to the next topic.

Dora said she saw her husband hand Conlee a wad of extorted money. It was in an envelope given to Sambo by a club operator, she said.

But Dora and the others were just preliminaries. The courtroom was really waiting for Sambo Hughes. When Sambo took the stand, Coolidge pulled his own chair directly in front of him. He stared at Sambo, but Sambo wouldn't look back. Coolidge was old now and ragged, and he couldn't stare down his old friend.

The bulky deputy would cry on the stand. He swore he was finally just telling the truth, something he said Conlee had never done. He lied to the grand jury when he denied extorting black nightclub operators, he said. But now he was coming clean for the people of his county.

Liz Jones, an office worker in the sheriff's department and a witness for the defense, tried to discredit Hughes by saying the chief deputy ran the department.

"Everyone felt like they would be fired if they bucked Sambo," she said. She also admitted she had accompanied Conlee on a trip to Las Vegas and that he had given her money and gifts.

Mrs. Jones said Hughes bragged that a psychiatric test he took to qualify for the deputy sheriff's position showed he had a "criminal mind." Hughes denied bragging about that, but he said when Conlee learned he had failed the test, the sheriff tore it up and had Hughes take another one. This time he passed.

Hughes told the jury he was not testifying against Conlee just to get less time in prison, as Easley implied. Hughes broke down. "I wanted to tell the jury what I'm guilty of, what I've done, and I know I'll have to face a penalty."

He said Conlee, as the two men were driving to Mississippi to recover some stolen goods in 1983, came up with the scheme to extort black nightclub owners. The sheriff knew gambling was going on at the clubs and saw an opportunity to make a few bucks. The sheriff, said Hughes, told him to tell the club operators: "If you play, you pay."

For about a year, six clubs paid $100 to $500 a week, Hughes swore. Conlee got two-thirds of the money and Hughes kept a third. When club operator Jesse Baldwin refused to cough up $500, Conlee told Hughes to "muscle" Baldwin. It was a shakedown, just as the club operators would testify. The money they paid, they said, was called "shake."

When Easley told him under cross-examination that he had abused his office, Hughes began to openly cry. "That's why I'm here. To set the record straight for St. Francis County."

A day later, Conlee followed his former colleague to the same witness chair from which he had been accused. With an exaggerated limp he wobbled forward, put his hand on the Bible, then climbed the two steps up. He sat down. He was sixty-four years old.

Against his better judgment, Hill was in the audience. Charlie Thompson, who had flown down for the trial, and his wife had convinced him to come. As soon as he walked in the courthouse, what he was afraid would happen, happened. A TV reporter screamed, "Do you feel vindicated, Jack?"

"I'm not the one on trial," he replied and kept moving. He hated to be uncooperative with those in his old profession, but the focus was now on Conlee and it should remain there, he thought.

Conlee was inarticulate on the stand. It was sad, but he made it so. He said Sambo was a liar; Dan Malone was a liar; Dora Hughes was a liar. He said others had misunderstood him. The people who had been facing the marijuana charge were told only of possible bond amounts. They mistakenly thought he was asking for a bribe, he said.

He paused frequently during his testimony to adjust his dentures.

The sheriff testified that he had heard Hughes was "on the take," and he spied on Sambo to catch him, but never could. "He outsmarted me," he said.

Conlee admitted to a fondness for gambling and that he had played dice in the sheriff's office before. But he didn't think it was illegal unless the house took a cut off the games. "With God as my witness, I'm telling the truth," Conlee said. It was an eerie paraphrase of Dumond's denial of the rape, when he had been on trial in Forrest City.

"I'm not an actor, I can't get up here and act like Mr, Hughes did—I'm telling the truth, After listening to the testimony, I can see where I made a mistake by keeping him."

Jack Hill thought Easley had made a mistake by putting the frail, wiry, poorly spoken country man up there, for all the world to see. The denials just did not wash. Apparently Easley wasn't such a tough adversary, Hill thought. He looked nice—a new haircut, a fine suit, and a shoeshine. But he reminded Jack of the "pretty boy" TV anchors. They performed well, but he had to wonder what was underneath the mousse.

Coolidge was on the stand for about three hours. Jack believed Conlee had sealed his fate.

The closing arguments were almost painful to watch. Hill, in the audience as Banks rose to make his final arguments, wondered whether anyone really knew what was at stake. Jack's own investments—his career, his home, his livelihood, his well-being—were less important than the practical considerations for St. Francis County. An innocent verdict would send a signal to the power hungry that they could rule with impunity. But a guilty verdict—that would help close the chapter on the county's most painful period; it would cleanse souls; it would help the good people of the county put behind them the years of agony, of helplessness, of loss.

For Banks, who likened himself to a country lawyer with a penchant for Arkansawyerisms (he pledged when taking the U.S. attorney's office not to forget "the folks who live on gravel roads"), the stakes were equally important. Nothing less than his future was on the line. He was politically ambitious and had run a high-profile race for Congress, which he had lost. But he seemed to be a rising star in the thin ranks of Arkansas Republicans. In such a highly publicized case, a political career could be lost.

It was strange how all the people had converged in this

courtroom, so many who had seen years of their lives tied up in the shenanigans of Coolidge Conlee:

Jack Hill, the TV anchorman and crusader.

His wife Anne, first a reluctant hero, now a front-line soldier.

Charlie Thompson, the tough producer for a powerful network news show.

Randy Little, the investigating officer who helped bring Conlee down.

Banks and aide Michael Johnson, the prosecutors.

Easley, Conlee's attorney who was trying to make his own name.

The scowling, owlish Judge Eisele.

Sambo and his wife, Dora, who had seen their lives take a sour turn.

Conlee himself, now frail and almost pathetic.

And one man who was not present should not be forgotten. He was not a whole man. His name was Wayne Dumond.

Now it was all coming to an end. Banks rose and walked toward the jury box. He stated the evidence against Conlee, but he didn't dwell on it. Instead, his would be an emotional summation, a tribute to the power that the Conlee case held over all.

The sheriff, Banks said, "has an enormous capacity to make people like and trust him. There's no better actor in this court this morning than the man who acted like he was sheriff of St. Francis County." Conlee was guilty, Banks said, not just of simple crimes but of betraying the public trust. The sheriff's only choice was to roll the dice one more time in the court of law.

The federal prosecutor, pacing now, ridiculed the idea

that Conlee was too simple or naive to catch Sambo in the act. Although the evidence showed he was hundreds of thousands of dollars in debt, the few hundred he got from shakedowns and dice rolling was important, Banks said. "You have that cash money so you can buy necklaces and take women to Las Vegas and offer them cars. You can play the hot-shot role, you see, 'cause you got that cash money in your pocket."

There was only one conclusion the jury could draw, Banks said, building to a climax. Conlee was crooked and had abused his power. Jabbing his finger at the wiry little man in the suit who once carried a badge, Banks said, "He makes a mockery of the system of government that gave him that badge because on the other side of that badge is sleaze!"

Someone gasped. He practically yelled it—sleaze. Easley sat looking at him in disbelief.

Then Banks stared straight at the jury. The matters before them were of the moment far beyond the tall walls of that courtroom, he said. The people of Arkansas were waiting for an answer.

Easley followed Banks to approach the jury box. The young attorney, with crisp suit and conservative tie, tried to punch holes in the government's case by pointing out that it was almost entirely built upon what Sambo Hughes had said— Hughes, an admitted thief and liar, someone testifying to save his own neck.

But the government had erred in bargaining with him, Easley said: "They made a deal with the Devil." Hughes, it was obvious, was the real center of the corruption in the sheriff's office, he said. The government had failed to prove Conlee was involved.

"I can't for the life of me figure out why they brought this case to trial, except that they got a Judas to sell out. A sheriff is what they want and a sheriff is what the media wants. They got somebody to sell out so they could get this shining target—a sheriff."

Friendly dice games at the sheriff's office didn't amount to racketeering, he said. Shakedowns of nightclub owners were done by Hughes, he said. He said the government's case fell like a house of cards if you removed the joker.

"I was proud to represent Coolidge Conlee from the beginning, and I'm proud to represent him now," he said.

He walked back to his leather high-back chair, sat down, leaned forward on his elbows and buried his face in his hands. It was almost as if he were praying.

The judge read the court's instructions to the jury on the matters of law, and they began deliberating. It was a little after noon on a Saturday in early November.

As a house gambler in Hot Springs, Coolidge wore eyeshades. He loved to shoot craps, loved to watch those dice fly. The casinos made him high. But the past was long over for Mr. C. He was trapped in the present, in a hallway in Little Rock's federal court building, near the drinking fountain, waiting for the jury to reach its verdict. Still, he couldn't resist talking about his Hot Springs heyday, and bystanders watched his eyes light up as he returned in his mind to the times of hot gambling, fast women, and cool money.

He remembered being a pit boss in Hot Springs, and the time he left the Vapors lounge shortly before a bomb went off in the restroom. "That was when the mob was trying to take over," he said.

Then there was the old saw about a man who came

into a club with a pistol and threw a few dice. If the stick man called seven a loser, he announced shortly, someone was going to be shot. The stick man didn't say a word, Conlee recalled, his eyes twinkling. "He just threw the stick on the table and walked out. I haven't seen him since."

It was well after lunch. Conlee's musings were interrupted by a knock on the jury room door. The jury had reached its verdict.

Conlee sat quietly as the jury filed in. Anne Hill, Charlie Thompson, and the federal agents who had investigated the case all held their breaths in the courtroom pews. Jack wasn't there. A rabid football fan, he decided he'd rather watch the Arkansas Razorbacks play for a Southwest Conference championship than sweat out a jury's deliberations.

In the courtroom, no one noticed that he was gone. All eyes were on the foreman, who handed the piece of paper to the bailiff, who carried it to Judge Eisele. Eisele opened the paper, read it silently, nodded, and handed it back to the bailiff.

The bailiff read the counts out one by one. Then the word came out—guilty.

Randy Little, the boyish-faced Alcohol, Tobacco and Firearms agent who had seen this case through the tedious dog days, buried his face. The courtroom sighed. All eight counts—guilty.

In the crush of reporters and photographers in the federal court hallway, Thompson yelled a question at Easley, the losing attorney.

"Don't you owe an apology to Jack Hill?"

"No!"

"Why not? He was right."

"I'll tell you why not. Jack Hill paid off people to defame Gene Raff and the circuit judge in the county." The allegation, Easley admitted later, was false. It was made in the heat of battle. Thompson couldn't help but rub it in.

The football game ended. The Hogs won the Southwest Conference title. Hill went back down to the courthouse. He saw a TV truck, ready for a live shot.

He swung around the corner, parked, and started for the back door. As he walked toward the building, someone called his name. He turned and saw Anne on the rear steps of John Hall's office, just a block away. She disappeared inside as he walked over. He was worried. Why had she not waited for him to tell him the verdict? Wouldn't she have yelled the news if Conlee had lost?

He burst into Hall's office. Anne, Charlie, Hall, and others were grinning and holding beers. He knew before they could speak—Conlee was guilty.

Jack had known it all along. It just took a trial for the rest of Arkansas to know. He sighed. Maybe, just maybe, the terror in the Delta was coming to an end.

That night in a bar near the courthouse, in downtown Little Rock, Charlie Thompson bought the drinks and ordered hors d'oevres. Anne and Charlie snacked on peanuts and goldfish crackers.

Randy Little came in. He was relieved and it showed on his face. Somebody asked him about the people who had died during the investigation—Osterman, the man who could have testified against Conlee—wasn't he suspicious?

Little just laughed. "You have to understand," he said. "We've been at this a long time. People die. Things change.

Life and death goes on." He shook his head. "We've been at this a very, very long time."

That night, on the news, instead of calling Coolidge Conlee a former sheriff, they called him a convicted felon.

Twenty-Five

This is one of the most serious crimes that can be committed.

—Judge G. Thomas Eisele

Two and a half weeks before Christmas, 1988, Conlee was back in the same courtroom standing before Federal Judge Eisele. He faced a lot of time and he knew it. His attorneys argued that, because he was ailing, a long sentence would amount to the death penalty. Conlee had written a letter to the judge saying he was wrongly convicted, that he was innocent.

A liar to the end, Hill thought.

The pleas didn't do any good. Eisele, who had heard all he wanted to hear about Conlee through the testicle case and the criminal case, was stern as he looked down.

231

> This is one of the most serious crimes that can be com-
> mitted. We're dealing with the abuse of the public trust.
> . . . The law gives certain people power and expects them
> to utilize it in a certain way. When it's used to break the
> law, it's one of the most heinous crimes.
>
> Here you have an officer of the law shaking down
> the most vulnerable people in the community for gambling,
> when in the sheriff's office gambling is being conducted
> every day. . . . I really cannot express adequately my
> feelings about this case. It casts a cloud over all law en-
> forcement. It brings into disrepute all law enforcement.

With that, he passed sentence. Twenty years. Conlee
would have to serve for at least seven years, until he was
more than seventy years old, before being eligible for parole.
And he knew what was ahead of him. A sheriff in jail faced
hatred, contempt, and retribution—every day.

Eisele didn't bother to impose a fine, which could have
amounted to $1 million. The judge noted that Conlee was
broke and $400,000 in debt, and a fine would be pointless.

Conlee's former friend and chief deputy, Sambo Hughes,
got a similar lecture from Eisele, and a nine-year sentence.

On March 6, 1989, nearly four years to the day after
Dumond was castrated, Conlee reported to the Fort Worth,
Texas, correctional facility, a medium security unit. Even-
tually, he was transferred to Texarkana, Texas.

As Conlee was going into prison, Wayne Dumond tried to
stay focused on getting out. It was his only goal. Once he
got out, he said:

The possibilities are unlimited. When I was out and had
a good job, I used to think, I couldn't do any better, I
couldn't better myself. I had a good job. Meantime the
whole world was out there, and I couldn't see the
possibilities. I couldn't see the trees for the forest. Now
I have had these years to set here, to think, to dwell, to
learn, to experience. . . .

I'm ready to go out and have a productive life.

He remembered his early days in prison. A Class 4
troublemaker, he had petitioned to be a Class 3. They laughed
at him.

He had tried suicide again. This time he shot saliva into
his foot. It swelled up as big as a baseball. "Man, I wish
I hadn't a done that." But he survived, again. He always
had such rotten luck.

But he learned. He became better at obeying the rules.
Eventually, he began to blend into the prison walls.

Charlie Thompson had been working on his piece for "20/
20" for more than three years, such a long time that in late
1988, when he told his bosses the piece would be ready
by the end of the year, they asked which year. But Conlee's
conviction gave him an excuse to air it. On January 13, 1989,
the segment finally saw the light of day.

Barbara Walters and Hugh Downs introduced it. Tom
Jarriel was the reporter. It ran on ABC as "The Law and
Sheriff Conlee." The program gave never-before publicized
details, such as the "Mr. C." comment, the identity of the
rape victim's father, and the funeral home's connection to
the jar of formaldehyde used to preserve Dumond's testicles.

Hill thought the lead-in newspaper accounts of the story

should have been, "ABC's '20/20' has linked former St. Francis County Sheriff Coolidge Conlee to the castration of Wayne Dumond. . . ." But of course, the print reporters didn't see it like that. The *Arkansas Gazette* went so far as to headline its story "Nothing new in program on '20/20.' "

What happened? Hill wondered. But he knew, really. It was the same thing that had happened to the news media throughout the Wayne Dumond story. They had abandoned the larger truths just to make it through the day. Hill was dismayed, but by now he was used to it.

Dumond was now working in prison as a tutor. He helped young men who were illiterate, or nearly so, to read. One of Dumond's students was a punk without a reason. Just for the hell of it he told Larry Lewis—an old thug in Forrest City who lived near Dumond in 19 Barracks—that Dumond said Lewis was one of the men who castrated him. Wayne remembered, "He done blew up. I have never felt so threatened in my whole life. Here comes Larry Lewis and this little punk behind him. He says, 'Man, I gotta talk to you.' " He threatened Dumond, but Dumond said the punk was a liar, and Lewis eased off.

The episode was fitting. Dumond was still in prison, no matter what they did to Coolidge. He was a prisoner to thugs and liars. His misery was continuing. Before he could hope to get out, he would have to tangle with the King of Arkansas. His name was Bill Clinton.

Twenty-Six

Just because I'm in national politics doesn't mean I'm going
to let exposés govern what I think is right or wrong.

—Bill Clinton

Whatever happened to justice?

—*Arkansas Democrat* editorial

In prison, you develop a routine. You have to to keep your
sanity. This became Dumond's routine:

Up at 6 A.M., teeth brushed, face washed, coffee downed.
He ate a cake each day for breakfast, because he didn't get
up early enough for prison breakfast. Early chow was 4
A.M. and he never could get up that early.

He cleaned his area. He did hobby crafts, including
making the clowns, and put his stuff on his bed so

235

maintenance crews wouldn't be bothered by it.

At 7 he went to school to tutor and got his first student at 7:30. At 9:10 he picked up another student, who would stay until 11. He then went to lunch until 1:30. An afternoon student would stay until 3. Afterwards, he went back to his barracks, where he would read and write letters. He wrote every day. In the barracks he made dolls. He talked and kicked back.

"I don't dip into other people's business. That's the best way to get into trouble. What I do is my business. What they do is their business. If they don't come dippin' in mine, I don't worry about them."

By January of 1989, he was forced to try his luck in federal court; his state avenues were exhausted. He had hope, but not much. Twice a federal court hearing was held on matters related to the new genetic evidence.

In one of the hearings, the victim repeated her identification of Dumond as the rapist, but Moses Schanfield, the Atlanta geneticist, said her story simply could not be true. Schanfield explained that he tested the semen taken from the pants leg—semen that the woman had said she spit there after Dumond forced her to have oral sex—and it did not match Dumond's. Since that semen was pure semen (because its mixture with her saliva did not taint it), there was only one conclusion—the semen wasn't Dumond's. However, Schanfield did say there was another possibility—that the girl wasn't telling the truth, that the semen had somehow been tainted through mixture with her vaginal fluids. In that case, he said, her story was wrong.

The U.S. Magistrate hearing the case, David Young, was not impressed. Twice he turned down a new trial for Dumond based on the new evidence. He said the woman's identification of Dumond was so strongly stated that a jury might well cast aside the genetic evidence and go with her word instead. The U.S. Circuit Court of Appeals was also of little help. It gave him no relief.

Hall and aide Craig Lambert tried another tack. They argued that Dumond's sentence—life plus twenty years—was excessive and far beyond what others convicted of similar crimes had received in St. Francis County. To prove their point, Hall and Lambert examined the records of every person charged in St. Francis County with rape or other sex offenses during the 1980s and compared the sentences with those charged with murder. "The results of this analysis are shocking and a disgrace to the American system of criminal justice," they wrote the federal court. Their conclusions:

- If Dumond's life sentence had been commuted to 100 years, as some states do, his total sentence of 120 years would exceed the total of all other sentences for sex crimes during the decade.

- Of all persons originally charged with rape and sentenced to jail, the average term was 6.5 years.

- The average term of all persons sentenced for first degree murder was 3.8 years.

"Life is cheap in St. Francis County; life is cheaper than one's sexual integrity," Hall and Lambert said. "On a relative scale of societal values, one would think that murder is a relatively more serious crime than rape, since a life is lost. In St. Francis County 1980-89, one was far better off to commit a cold-blooded murder than to force a woman to submit to sexual intercourse."

They said Dumond was singled out for strict punishment because his victim was white, wealthy, and from a politically well-connected family. They pointed out that the victim's father was a fraternity brother of Raff and Long, as well as a longtime friend of Long.

In a "remarkably similar" case that Lambert and Hall studied, in which the victim was abducted in daylight, driven to a wooded area, raped orally and vaginally, and returned to the abduction site, the accused was allowed to plead to a reduced charge of first-degree sexual assault. "A big difference between that case and this case is that his victim was poor, pregnant, black, and without political influence," they wrote.

The magistrate in this round of appeals, Henry Jones, Jr., ruled that Dumond just didn't have grounds for his arguments. He said those claims should have been made in state court. Again, the rejection of Dumond's plea was made on procedural grounds. Whether it was true made no difference.

Dumond still had a few other chances for federal court appeals, but by now it was painfully obvious to even the most casual observer that something was wrong with the system. The *Arkansas Democrat,* in supportive editorials, railed against failures of the courts to come to terms with what had been a patently unfair ordeal. Dumond had been arrested, castrated, and tried in the same county, a county with a corrupt sheriff who was ruled over by a prosecutor who had been rebuked in federal court for selective prosecution. The father of Dumond's alleged victim was close to that prosecutor. Dumond's genetic evidence was never admitted. New evidence cast serious doubt on the victim's story. How could anyone not see that Dumond did not receive a fair trial? How could this injustice be tolerated?

All that didn't matter to the courts. The narrow interests of the law did not extend to the principles of justice.

Dumond's setbacks in federal court left him in despair. It was almost worse, really, to have no hope than to continually have his hopes raised, only to see them dashed.

He knew he couldn't count on the governor by asking for clemency. He thought Clinton's relation to the victim's family made him prejudiced, and the governor had shown no willingness to get involved. However, there was a way to put pressure on Clinton. Hall took Dumond's case to the Arkansas Board of Pardons and Paroles.

At first glance, that chance appeared equally slim. All the members of the parole board had been appointed by Clinton, who had been governor for nearly a decade. Many were allies of the governor. It seemed unlikely that they would go against his wishes.

Yet on June 27, 1990, the head of the parole board, Mike Gaines, announced that the board had unanimously recommended the immediate release of Dumond. Gaines said Dumond's case was "a miscarriage of justice." Gaines said the reasons for recommending clemency were twofold: the atmosphere surrounding Dumond's trial and the severity of his sentence. Although clemency was not a clearing of Dumond's record—only a governor's pardon would do that—it was better than nothing. Still, clemency could not be granted without Clinton's approval. The board's position was just a recommendation.

The decision left both sides in shock. The rape victim's mother said Dumond was dangerous and should never be released. Dusty, though, said in a telephone interview to a reporter:

> I've been turning somersaults, singing and dancing. I'm deliriously happy.
>
> I'm looking forward to putting on my yellow dress with a yellow rose and putting yellow ribbons 'round the old oak tree. I'm really believing they'll set him free, exonerate his name. I wouldn't be defending a man to help him get away with rape. He was the one who's been raped. He lost his wife, his home, his manhood, and five years of his life. But I pray for her [the victim]. I don't hate her. I just don't understand how one girl and one lie could destroy an entire family.

Hall said he would go to Clinton and ask for swift action. He said he did not want Clinton to recuse himself from the case, even though Clinton was related to the victim. "He's the one that asked to be governor, and he's the one who was elected," Hall said.

Clinton did react swiftly—the next day he said he wouldn't act on the board's recommendation while Dumond still had appeals pending. Under questioning from reporters, Clinton said that the rape victim's great-grandfather and his own step-grandmother were brother and sister. But that had nothing to do with his consideration of the case, he said—even though he remained close to the victim and her family.

Hall, in a press conference in his book-lined library, was hopping mad and he showed it. "I think it's premature for him to say that, since he hasn't seen the paperwork." Noting that an election was coming up in November of that year

(Clinton was seeking re-election), Hall said Dumond is "literally becoming a political prisoner because no one wants to do anything until November." He went on, his tone rising:

> I expected more out of Bill Clinton than this kind of crap. The case before the Eighth Circuit is an entirely independent issue. He's got shallow thinking. He used to be attorney general. Where's his mind? Wayne Dumond isn't the only man without balls.

A month later, after who-knows-what behind-the-scenes manipulations, the parole board caved in. In an unprecedented move, it revoked its earlier stand and asked Clinton to return Dumond's file so it could reconsider the case. "We do not live in a vacuum," parole-board head Gaines said. "We know what publicity this has received."

The *Arkansas Democrat* knew all about politics and Wayne Dumond. In an editorial headlined, "Politics vs. Justice," the newspaper said:

> Raw political power on the part of Gov. Bill Clinton, it seems, will evidently keep Wayne Dumond in the penitentiary despite dark clouds of doubt that continue to hover over his conviction for the rape of a Forrest City teenager.
>
> Whatever happened to justice? Laboratory analysis has shown that Dumond's semen did not genetically match the semen specimen taken from the victim's clothing.
>
> And what about justice for the two still-unidentified men who broke into Dumond's home and castrated him while he was awaiting trial?
>
> As for Dumond, reasonable doubt is all that it takes for a jury to acquit someone of a crime, but post-conviction relief by members of the parole board appears subject to

the views of the governor who appointed them.

When the members unanimously recommended clemency, they obviously thought Dumond deserved relief. But when the governor refused to act, his own staff helped the victim's lawyers draft the rehearing petition, and the board knuckled under.

Why did Clinton do it? For one thing he is a . . . cousin of the rape victim—and close to politically prominent St. Francis County people who opposed clemency for Dumond.

It would be fatuous for Clinton to pretend that his family and political ties to the Dumond case didn't influence his opposition to the parole board's recommendation of clemency in June. . . .

But last week, in response to the board's reneging, Clinton came clean, declaring, "I am just not going to grant clemency based on that fact that [Dumond] served four years and ten months. They think that's too long. I don't."

We do and countless others think it's enough.

John R. Starr, a nemesis of Clinton and a columnist for the *Democrat*, chimed in.

The governor doesn't care whether justice is done in the Dumond case. He does not intend to put himself into the position of having to look his distant relative and good friend in the eye and tell her, "I let the man who raped you go free."

The quality of mercy is strained through family relationships.

If Clinton becomes a lifetime governor—and he can if he wants to be—Wayne Dumond's only hope of getting out of prison is the federal courts, and I'm not sure he has a leg to stand on there.

After Clinton took this skewering from his home-state press, the parole board held a full hearing on Dumond's case. The first part of it was held in Forrest City. Fletcher Long, the victim, and her family were on hand. For the third time, the woman testified that Dumond raped her. She said she feared for her life if he was let free.

At Cummins, the board held the second part of the hearing. Dumond, for the umpteenth time, said he had nothing to do with the rape. "They tied me up, they forced me to the floor . . . they castrated me. . . . If I ever owed the state anything, if I ever had a debt to society, it's paid."

The board also heard the echoes of Dumond's past. The other woman who had originally said Dumond raped her—then dropped the charges—came forward and said she had been assaulted by him. Dumond was fearsome, she said. Dumond told the board that he did have sex with her, but it was consensual.

In September, the second parole board ruling came down. This time it wasn't as favorable for Dumond, but it was still better than what he had faced before. The parole board recommended Dumond's sentence be commuted. Simply put, it meant that the board wanted the sentence reduced, but the recommendation fell short of the previous request that he be freed immediately. Three parole board members said the sentence should be commuted to thirty years, one voted for commutation without specifying a term, and another said Dumond's sentence should be limited to time served.

Clinton's comment:

I'm not sure what their reasoning is, but the most important thing to me is that this man has appeals left to be pursued and I have not ever commuted anybody's sentence with their appeals proceeding, as far as I know.

From Forrest City, Long took another shot.

Why should the governor commute it to a term of thirty years? [Dumond] has showed absolutely no remorse. He has shown nothing to me to show he's done anything to rehabilitate himself. I think Governor Clinton has got better sense than that. I don't think he's going to do it. I don't think parole boards serve to second-guess juries.

Throughout this portion of Dumond's ordeal, Bill Clinton was Dumond's key hurdle. So it was strange that Dumond's biggest break came when Clinton began successfully seeking the nation's highest office. Clinton, who had hemmed and hawed about the case, finally did the right thing when he decided to run for president. Realizing that his distant relation to the rape victim was potentially a conflict of interest, he turned the case over to Jim Guy Tucker, Arkansas' swift-talking, swift-thinking lieutenant governor. Tucker assumed the powers of the governor whenever Clinton was out of state, which, as soon as Clinton began his race for the presidency, was most of the time.

Clinton stormed into Houston on October 10, 1991, to try to bolster his chances for one of the biggest prizes—the Texas delegation to the Democratic Convention. Clinton went to a local health clinic and touted health care reform, a key issue that helped him win the White House and one that his wife, Hillary, would later command.

Clinton was looking for money, votes, and support for

the health-reform idea. What he got was an earful from a Houston woman who confronted him on a Houston street. Debbie Riddle, a Houston political activist, asked the governor about Wayne Dumond.

"He's already served longer than others like him," she said.

"That's not true," Clinton shot back.

Riddle mentioned that the Dumond case had become something of a cause célèbre on tabloid TV shows, but Clinton said he would stand his ground. "Just because I'm in national politics doesn't mean I'm going to let exposés govern what I think is right or wrong."

To reporters who would listen to her, Riddle said she had become a friend of Dusty and the Dumond family and she believed the whole issue should be "a thorn in [Clinton's] saddle." "I intend to make everyone in Texas aware of Governor Clinton's insensitivity toward an innocent man," she said. She said Clinton "can't see the case objectively" because of his relation to the victim's family.

Aides gently turned Clinton away from Riddle, and he talked to reporters instead. Her "thorn" didn't do a lot of good. Clinton swept Texas on his way to the nomination.

Only Clinton knows whether he surrendered control of the case to Tucker because he was concerned it could hurt him in his foray into national politics. What is certain is that the case wasn't even a blip on the campaign trail. "20/20" aired its report on Coolidge Conlee again once Clinton entered the race, pointing out Clinton's relation to the victim; a slew of tabloid television programs reported on Dumond's trials; Dusty Dumond made it her business to protest Clinton's lack of attention to her husband's plight by trying to get national coverage whenever and wherever possible. None of this made the slightest difference in Democratic primaries as Clinton marched toward the nomination.

Though Anne and Jack had heard it was coming down, it was still somewhat of a shock when they heard the news on tax day, April 15, 1992: Acting Governor Tucker commuted Dumond's life-plus-twenty-year prison sentence to thirty-nine and a half years, The commutation came just hours after a still-hoarse Clinton, who had suspended his campaign for six days to let his throat recover from stump-speech rhetoric, left Arkansas and turned over the state's reins to Tucker. The commutation made Dumond eligible for parole in 1995.

Immediately there was outrage, but not from Clinton. The governor's office issued a statement saying he agreed with Tucker's action. After that statement, the Arkansas press corps wanted to ask Clinton, "Then why didn't you do what Tucker did?" But they couldn't. He was unavailable for comment. And the national press wasn't interested enough in the issue to bring it up to candidate Clinton.

Tucker said Dumond's castration had played a major factor in his decision. "Regardless of who was responsible, this was a reprehensible action which no society can condone," Tucker wrote to John Hall. "It seems clear that it was intended to be extrajudicial, vigilante punishment of Mr. Dumond for the crime with which he had been charged." He said he discussed it with Clinton, but would say no more. The victim's father said the action was a setback to every woman who was raped.

Even Dusty wasn't entirely pleased. "I'm disappointed in a way. I was hoping for immediate relief. But we see the light at the end of the tunnel and this time it isn't a train." She had tried to stop the Clinton juggernaut to the nomination. But she realized by now, April, that she was fighting something bigger than she was. "When he gets the nomination, the Republican Party will eat him alive for this," she said. It was a pathetic hope from a tiny little voice. Then she added, "All I'm going to pray for now is to see Wayne come home and forget about ruining Clinton."

Tucker said a key point was that Dumond's jurors were not allowed to consider his castration while they were deliberating the case. "I have to suspect that if you are going to sentence someone to the penitentiary for rape and you were permitted to consider he had been castrated, that would enter into your mind." Perhaps the reasoning was a little tortured—anyone familiar with the law knew that the facts of the castration weren't relevant to the rape—but the effect was the same. For the first time, Dumond knew that he would someday go free.

However, that didn't stop Forrest City state Representative Pat Flanagin, brother-in-law of Sambo Hughes, from jumping into the fray. Although most would have thought Flanagin might have had enough of Dumond, Conlee, and the whole bit when his sister, Dora Flanagin Hughes, had been forced to testify at Conlee's federal trial and, by her own admission, embarrass herself, he went right to Tucker with the rape victim's father. The castration, Flanagin said, "had something to do with a misfortune that came into his life, either at his own hand or someone else's. It had nothing to do with the crime and had nothing to do with the sentence."

Whatever point Flanagin may have had was thrown out the window by his repetition of Conlee's old saw about Dumond possibly castrating himself. But the victim's father scored when he pointed out to Tucker that his action may have made rape victims afraid to come forward and accuse their assailants. He said it proved that the criminal justice system too often protected criminals at the expense of victims.

Tucker said he sympathized with the victim's father. "If I was in his position, I would want to kill the guy," he said. Still, he said he believed a vigilante attack warranted a reduced sentence. His decision would stand.

That day, Tucker also issued a proclamation celebrating Crime Victim Rights Week in Arkansas.

All these events took their toll on the rape victim. In her first newspaper interview since the rape, she told the *Arkansas Democrat* that the ordeal had exacted a terrible price. Still, she said, she stood by her story.

As the story by reporter William Green put it:

> Sitting on a long sofa in the den of the family's white-columned home east of Forrest City, the dark-haired, brown-eyed young woman, who wore black bermuda shorts and a white sweatshirt, expressed no anger or other extreme outward emotion. Rather, she spoke softly, almost shyly, and appeared happy, adjusted, thoughtful and interested in the world around her. Her mother sat in a chair across the room, occasionally offering comments. . . .
>
> She only alluded to the trauma she suffered, saying she overcame it with the support of her family, and the strength she had gained from her upbringing. "I've always been taught: no matter what, life goes on; you can't let anything get you down."

Twenty-Seven

You take a wheel. And this wheel is your life.

—Wayne Dumond

In his own way, Sambo Hughes had become a hero, because he finally turned away from his friend and boss, Coolidge Conlee. He wanted to turn his life around, said the federal prosecutor, and he did.

Wayne Dumond had also been a hero, long ago. He thought often about that time in Cambodia, when he had saved his unit from the bombing. But becoming a hero wasn't to be his fate. Instead, when he returned to the states, he became a criminal. That first rape charge did him in. Surely the cops had found that charge when he was accused of the second rape. Surely that's what made him a scapegoat. He would never be separated from that past. They had taken him from society, locked him in the hole, severed him from his life and family—but he would never be severed from that past.

In prison, a reporter once asked Dumond why he'd been such a target of misfortune, why he seemed to look for trouble.

"I haven't been in so much trouble," he said in that Delta-soaked backwoods drawl. "I've just had a few bad experiences. Wrong crowd. I've also had some wonderful experiences." He went on:

> Think about it like this. You take a wheel. And this wheel is your life. As long as everything is balanced, it'll spin and you keep rollin' and everything's okay. But what happens if on one side of that wheel—let's say too much good gets over here on one side of this wheel, and it starts to get things outa balance. You're gonna have to get something over here, maybe some bad, to counteract it. I'm not sayin' there's been too much good and there had to be some bad for me. But maybe there was some bad and there had to be some good to counteract that. The wheel stays balanced, and it keeps turning, and I keep goin'.

For one night, he was the star of maximum security, when Thompson finally aired his report on Conlee, Hill, and Dumond. The inmates watched "20/20" in the barracks. They cheered. Dumond smiled.

He became the hero of the Cummins Unit.

Like Dumond, Jack Hill would spend many hours thinking about his strange journey. He had been to the dungeon and had returned. He too had been severed from what he loved. He came away a changed man. His faith in our system was shaken. He was no longer "Mr. TV Anchorman," and could never return to the suburbs. Instead he was more determined than ever to make a difference for people. He launched independent television projects on education and related issues that were important to ordinary people.

But Jack Hill was, and is, a religious man. He was never able to get over the Wayne Dumond case. He was often haunted by it; it has stayed with him. Perhaps it always will. Hill could only wonder: If Coolidge Conlee had been exposed sooner, would Dumond be free? Would he be whole?

He would write later:

> The Dumond case exposes fundamental flaws in the journalistic process which cause those involved to answer to narrow, self-serving considerations—and not to the common cause.
>
> We bellyache about the mindless routines of journalism, the filling of the news hole each day. And yet we're in love with that routine. It forms our agenda; it *is* our agenda. We'll decide what the news is, thank you, based on a predetermined, often arrogant set of priorities.
>
> Frequently these priorities have nothing to do with the public interest and serve only our egos, our insecurities, our thirst for short-term popularity.
>
> When confronted with an extraordinary situation like the Dumond case, we can't respond appropriately. We want to give a matter that, for the Delta, was Watergate-like in its scope, the same routine treatment to which we've grown accustomed.
>
> Dumond represents the ultimate failure of journalism—an innocent man who is castrated and locked away as his assailants go free—while journalism refuses to deal with the facts.

Surely, there must be some lessons here.

What good is a First Amendment if we don't use it? We live in a land in which speech critical of public officials is the most constitutionally protected, yet we ignore the facts, fearing a lawsuit. This goes far beyond a television station calling a reporter off a story. Sadly, the whole institution of journalism serving Arkansas quaked at the foot of a corrupt political machine. It was easy to just report a few court actions, to never dig to find the truth.

On the other hand, the Dumond story shows how valuable the media can be.

When Conlee was exposed, the people of St. Francis County went to the polls and threw the rascal out. They also summarily tossed out Gene Raff.

Given the information they need, citizens won't make many mistakes. But if information is withheld, people are blind.

Arkansas journalists are really no different from those anywhere else. They share the same pressures, the same deadlines, the same working environments.

So when a dangerous story comes along, journalists usually have no patience to deal with it. Dumond thus became a symbol of institutional failure. Journalism failed him, so the criminal justice system failed him. He did not have the constitutional protections to which we pay such lip service. And if Wayne Dumond does not have these protections, no one does.

Idealistic? Certainly. Democracy itself is an ideal. And it cannot work unless its journalism works.

In a state like Arkansas—so diverse, yet so illiterate and rural—television is the key. Unfortunately, television journalism in Arkansas was just an extension of the Great American Sellathon. The stations are just selling themselves.

In Little Rock, the attitude among TV news stations is simply, "We want you to like us, please like us." The anchors are reduced to handsome personalities, little more than deejays of TV.

Arkansas, though it ranks near the bottom of states, is much like other places. In fact, a lot of Arkansas's ideas about journalism have been imported, from places like Dallas or Chicago.

Wayne Dumond is no saint and never pretended to be, but there is a universality in what he represents—his case asks the question, "Will truth and justice ultimately prevail?"

It will prevail only to the extent that journalism does the job the Founding Fathers expected

When a man is severed from the rest of us, he is forced to consider the hideous. He is forced to face the truth. In prison, more than once in his mind, Wayne Dumond stared at that ugly truth. He was forced back to that room, just off the kitchen, in the modest country house on Crowley's Ridge outside Forrest City, in the isolated Delta of Arkansas. More than once he had relived it. In a sense he never left that room. He was imprisoned by it, just as surely as he was imprisoned in the barracks at the Arkansas Cummins Unit.

The blood. His blood. To be sure, it was at the center of his horror. But there was more than that. For so long he could not speak of it. The masked men. The distorted faces. For years he would think about them. He would think about that cocked pistol against his skull. He had no choice but to do what they said. It was probably good that he had been drinking that day. It might have lowered his defenses, but it also lowered his pain.

His shame had been so great after the attack that he had wanted it to stay out of the papers. No one had to know that his manhood was gone. He could almost laugh about that, years later. In prison those who knew him could joke about it. No scrotum there, just a tight piece of skin. His shame. Funny it had been directed at the loss of his balls in the moments and the days after. Slowly he began to realize that his shame was really about something else.

For something else had happened that day. He would have to face it. He would have to go back to that room.

Dumond didn't hear them coming. Maybe it was the Jim Beam. Maybe it was the accusation of rape. He was distracted. He was alone in his thoughts. When the front door burst open, he looked up, saw their stocking masks, and made the move for his gun rack. Of course he was stopped by the sound of the pistol cocking. Anyone would have been. He had no choice but to do what they said. He had no choice.

They ordered him down. One of them was chattering crazily. He held the gun. Down to his knees. In front of the big one. The man unzipped his fly. He pulled out his penis and stuck it in Dumond's face.

"Oh man, oh man."

"Suck it. Just like you made her do."

"Oh man."

"Do it!" The gun was hard against his temple. "Do it or I'll blow your fucking head off."

Dumond took the man's penis in his mouth.

"Suck it, suck it!"

Slowly it grew bigger. "Stroke it!"

Oh, he hated to face it. Oh how he hated those men.

It didn't take all that long. He ejaculated in Dumond's

mouth. Dumond spit it out.

That's when they laid him out, and put him to the knife. The blood mixed with the semen.

Dumond kept his secret with him until, in prison, he told a reporter what had really happened. He told it again before the Board of Pardons and Paroles. And not until that moment did he really feel released of his secret. Not until then did he really feel free from that room. For Wayne Dumond's severance went beyond his isolation from society, first in life, then in war, then in a drugged haze, then in prison, and in the solitary hole. His true severance had been from himself, and from the truth.

But his severance ended that day before the Board of Pardons and Paroles. He faced what really happened. And finally, he became whole again.

Epilogue

Wayne's ability to put behind him that terrible day was a step forward for his whole family. When he told them everything that had happened, he truly was able to escape the dark cloud of his past.

Of course, his past had probably haunted him more than it did others. Though Wayne's own descriptions of his youthful indiscretions might have put off some women, Dusty would say later that she saw the good in the man. She saw a churchgoer, a good father, a gentleman. For Dusty, herself a loving mother and Christian woman with strong values and a solid sense of right and wrong, these good qualities matched her own values. They provided the foundation for what she believed would be a strong family. She could never have known that the family she worked so hard to bring together would be ripped apart by forces beyond her control.

But the Dumonds learned from their experiences, just

as life has hard lessons for us all. Today Dusty still uses the hardships she has endured as sources of strength as she continues to fight for her husband's freedom.

Partly because of the sacrifices of Jack and Anne Hill, there is a rebirth among the downtrodden of the Delta, where blacks are winning legislative races and the white collars finally outnumber the red necks. The Delta is truly part of the emerging New South, and it isn't just because Arkansas finally gave birth to a president. Like so many areas that dot the Midwest and West, the Delta is given to old prejudices and hindered by past mistakes. But it is maturing in political consciousness and determined to come into its own.

Jack Hill and Wayne Dumond couldn't have been more different. One was a do-gooder, the other a ne'er-do-well. One smoked dope, the other never touched a drink. But they shared an odd fate in the Delta, for they came to symbolize the oppression that went hand-in-hand with the absolute corruption in East Arkansas.

Hill would never want to be called a hero, so suffice it to say that his actions in St. Francis County would have made his father, Radus Hill, proud. His actions in St. Francis County wouldn't have disappointed the namesake of St. Francis County, Francis of Assisi. For like St. Francis, Hill sacrificed his livelihood for a greater cause, the cause of the truth.

On April 24, 1990, Coolidge Conlee's life ended at Wadley Regional Medical Center in Texarkana, Texas. He was being held at the Federal Correctional Institution in Texarkana and was transferred to the hospital, where he suffered cardiac failure while undergoing open-heart surgery.

Conlee's obituary has to be one of the few in history that contained the word "testicles." *The Commercial Appeal* of Memphis noted in its story of his death, "Conlee had displayed Dumond's severed testicles on his desk. That incident helped bring the once powerful lawman down."

John Hall remarked, "It's always sad when somebody's family member dies, but all I can say is, it's fitting he died in prison." Hall couldn't resist another shot. The news of Conlee's death just wasn't that important, he said. "Conlee wasn't anything. All he was was a pissant sheriff."

Parkman, who took Conlee's place as sheriff of St. Francis County, had no comment.

Others were a little kinder. Everett Watson, who knew Conlee much of his life, said the sheriff was "really a likable fellow, if you knew him a little bit. He would go out of his way to help you. Of course, there were some things he'd do that I wouldn't approve of. Everybody always knew that he gambled, but that didn't bother most folks. I would vote for him today if I could."

Today

This book is not fiction, so the loose ends cannot be tied neatly into pretty packages:

Jack Hill is an independent film producer living with his wife *Anne* in Little Rock.

Wayne Dumond remains in prison. He has been transferred to the Wrightsville unit and is scheduled to be released in 1995.

Charlie Thompson became a producer for "60 Minutes."

After his re-election defeat, *Gene Raff* proved his political powerlessness by being trounced in an election to the board of a local community college. He lives in Helena, Arkansas.

The *rape victim* has lived in various cities in Arkansas. *Her father* still runs the funeral home in Forrest City.

Sambo Hughes has completed his federal prison term in Fort Worth, Texas.

On January 23, 1993, *Bill Clinton* became the nation's forty-second president. When he announced for the office in October, he promised families "a government that fights for them."

Dan Dane left the prosecuting attorney's office to pursue private business. He was succeeded by *Fletcher Long,* who has criticized the ineptitude of the office and vowed to make it run more efficiently.

Today there is no active investigation of Wayne Dumond's castration.

The fact that his attackers forced Dumond to perform oral sex—just as he had supposedly done to his victim—proved this was no random attack by vigilantes. Whoever castrated Dumond knew the girl's story—before Dumond ever went to trial. A few, Conlee included, knew that story. That proves very little, of course, but it was enough to make Dumond think. He had plenty of time to think.

Today the men who castrated Dumond walk free. Is there any hope that a local officer, or a local federal official, could revive the case? Is there any chance the president might? Is there any reason to believe that would make any difference? It is doubtful. The people who castrated Dumond probably will never be caught.

Meanwhile, Dumond is in a barracks in South Arkansas with fifty other men, waiting. We like to think that Dumond's

is an extraordinary case, but perhaps some of the other inmates' experiences with the criminal justice system aren't
so different. Who knows how many innocent men are behind
those bars? How many have been wrongly killed or maimed?
How many more will follow?

Acknowledgments

Thanks to the news media for being cooperative in bringing this story together, to investigating authorities who provided assistance, to Jack and Anne Hill for their perseverance, and to my father for his support. Special thanks to my agent, Janet Wilkens Manus, who had faith in this project from its inception.